MURDER
IN
AMERICA

To Tootie—my wife, Steve's mother
To Amy—Steve's wife, my grandkids' mother

SECOND EDITION

MURDER
IN
AMERICA

Ronald M. Holmes
Stephen T. Holmes

Sage Publications, Inc.
International Educational and Professional Publisher
Thousand Oaks ▪ London ▪ New Delhi

For information:

Sage Publications, Inc.
2455 Teller Road
Thousand Oaks, California 91320
E-mail: order@sagepub.com

Sage Publications Ltd.
6 Bonhill Street
London EC2A 4PU
United Kingdom

Sage Publications India Pvt. Ltd.
M-32 Market
Greater Kailash I
New Delhi 110 048 India

Printed in the United States of America

Library of Congress Cataloging-in-Publication Data

Holmes, Ronald M.
    Murder in America / by Ronald M. Holmes, Stephen T. Holmes —
2nd ed.
        p. cm.
    Includes bibliographical references and index.
    ISBN 0-7619-2091-9 (cloth: acid-free paper)
    ISBN 0-7619-2092-7 (pbk.: acid-free paper)
    1. Murder—United States. 2. Homicide—United States.
I. Holmes, Stephen T. II. Title.
    HV6529 .H664   2001
    364.15′23′0973—dc21   00-011614

01   02   03   04   05   06   07   7   6   5   4   3   2   1

Acquiring Editor:	Margaret H. Seawell/Jerry Westby
Editorial Assistant:	Heidi Van Middlesworth
Production Editor:	Denise Santoyo
Typesetter/Designer:	Lynn Miyata
Cover Designer:	Michelle Lee
Indexer:	Teri Greenberg

CONTENTS

PREFACE

Not a day passes when a murder is not reported. Obviously, the more bizarre the murder, the more attention the media devote to it. For example, when the Rafael Resendez-Ramircz case first came to the attention of the public, we, as experts on serial murder, were besieged by requests for television appearances, radio talk show engagements, and interviews, from California to Florida. For a day or two, we were hot property. Murder sells. However, in teaching university classes on homicide, we were somewhat surprised that we could not find an adequate text addressing the various forms of murder that we discussed in class. To this end, we decided to update a text that we wrote several years ago that still suits our purposes and is, we hope, useful, informative, and suitable for various classes at other colleges and universities. Some people might debate the types of homicide discussed, or not discussed, in this book. We have chosen to include the types of murder with which we have become most acquainted in our professional capacities as academicians and authors, and, in the case of the first author, as a deputy coroner. We have had the opportunity to offer assistance to police departments throughout the United States on more than 500 murder and rape cases. Most of these cases involved sexually motivated homicide, occult-related and ritualistic crimes, mass murder, and murder within families. Our choices also reflect the interests of our students, who, over the years, have indicated their desire for information about these forms of homicide. We believe that the types selected deserve special attention and consideration because they are not covered adequately in existing professional and academic publications. Thus, we include chapters that deal with atypical and relatively bizarre homicides, such as serial murder, mass murder, and terrorism and assassination. Other, more common, types of murder are discussed as well, such as murder committed by children, murder of children, partner homicide, and workplace homicides. The volume is divided into nine chapters that can be read in any order; each chapter is designed to stand alone.

Although we mention theories in passing throughout this book, our focus is on the pragmatic examination of selected forms of homicide, trends, methods, motives, statistics, and other descriptive information. Interested students are encouraged to seek out relevant theories in primary sources that offer more detailed discussion than we can include here. In addition to the numerous journal articles listed in our references, there are many books available, such as Lilly, Cullen, and Ball's (1989) *Criminological Theory: Context and Consequences,* that are valuable resources for serious students interested in pursuing further study of the forms of homicide included in this book.

Of course, no work of this type can be completed without the cooperation and understanding of a large number of people. Despite the obvious danger of forgetting someone when listing important contributors, we are willing to run that risk to thank the following people: Sergeant David Rivers, Metro-Dade (Florida) Police Department; Detective Jay Whitt, Greensboro (North Carolina) Police Department; Dr. Richard Greathouse, Coroner, Louisville, Kentucky; Dr. Eric Hickey, University of California at Fresno; Dr. Al Carlisle, psychologist at Utah State Prison; Dr. George Rush, California State University at Long Beach; Dr. Ed Latessa, James Frank, Frank Cullen, and Larry Travis of the University of Cincinnati; Drs. Bernie McCarthy, David Fabianic, and Elizabeth Mustaine of the University of Central Florida; Dr. Robert Langworthy of the National Institute of Justice, and Jim Massie, parole officer, State of Kentucky.

We also owe a great debt to our students. Their interest, questions, demands, and quizzical expressions keep us on our toes. They also keep us mentally alert and eager for the next class.

Finally, our families—especially our wives—deserve special attention. They are attentive to our interests, although they do not completely understand our enthusiasm for interviewing serial killers, attending autopsies, or visiting homicide scenes. It might be easier for them if our interests were different. Our wives are sometimes reluctant to answer telephones; on more than one occasion, they have answered when serial killers have called from prison, wanting to share some thoughts. To Tootie and Amy go our special thanks.

— *Ronald M. Holmes*
— *Stephen T. Holmes*

MURDER IN AMERICA

Murder captivates the interest of people all over the world, and no less here in the United States. This interest is reflected not only in our reading habits, but also in popular television programs and Hollywood movies. In the 1991 film *The Silence of the Lambs,* the main character tries to track down a serial murderer by getting inside the mind of convicted killer Hannibal Lecter; this movie became a national hit. The Rambo and Terminator characters and others in action movies further reflect our interest in the world of the violent.

The true character of murder is different from what is depicted in the media—in, for example, the Dirty Harry movies, movies about organized crime figures, and even the "reality programming" genre. In university classes on homicide investigation or the sociology of murder, students are visibly shaken when actual murder scenes are shown and cases discussed. When a teleconference call is made from one of our classes to a serial killer in prison for an interview, the students expect to hear a snarling, rabid murderer. Unexpectedly, he is soft-spoken and articulate—not at all what was expected. Scarcely, however, is murder what is expected.

Murder by children, homicide within the family, serial murder, mass murder, school shooters, murder in the workplace, and other forms of fatal violence are discussed in the chapters in this book. Undoubtedly, these types of homicides are reflective of our changing society, as well as of the changing values and attitudes within society. These changing norms, values, attitudes, and customs are examined here as they relate to acts of homicide.

MURDER: DEFINITIONS

Homicide and murder are synonyms. In an early work, Lunde (1977) defines murder as the unlawful killing of a human being with malice afore-thought (Lunde, 1977, p. 3). George Rush, a well-respected criminologist, defines homicide as "any willful killing" (Rush, 2000, p. 162). Our defini-tion of homicide is simple: The unlawful killing of a human being by another human being. Beirne and Messerschmidt (2000) define murder simply as the "willful killing of one human being by another, usually with premedita-tion" (p. 511). Swanson, Chamelin, and Terriro (1996) define murder as "the killing of a human being by another with malice aforethought" (p. 306). Regardless, it appears that homicide and murder are used inter-changeably by people within the criminal justice enterprise.

Many cases of homicide take place during the commission of other crimes. This distinction becomes important when one considers the two major types of murder. The first type is motivated by instrumental gain. Such murders are part of well-planned activities intended to result in the perpetrator's acquisition of power or property, such as business interests, money, or status. A second type of murder may be called impulsive homi-cide; it results from sudden action, such as a barroom brawl or other sudden confrontation. In the analysis of these two types of homicides, the location of motivation is the starting point for a discussion and analysis of homicide itself.

LEGAL DEGREES OF MURDER

Typically found in legal discussions of murder is a differentiation between murder in the first degree and murder in the second degree. First-degree mur-der has two major components: premeditation and deliberation. To qualify as murder in the first degree, a homicide must be considered beforehand. When attempting to establish first-degree murder, the prosecution must prove to the jury that the act was not spontaneous—that the accused considered the act before carrying it out. The second element is that of deliberation. This means that the murder was planned—even if only momentarily—and that it was not impulsive.

Murder in the second degree contains an element of malice beforehand, but no premeditation or deliberation. The type of malice is also considered in this definition. There are two types of malice: expressed and implied. Expressed malice exists when someone murders another in the absence of any apparent motivation. Implied malice exists when murder results from negligent or unthinking behavior on the part of the perpetrator.

MANSLAUGHTER

Manslaughter is the unlawful taking of a life without malice or the intent to do harm. Voluntary manslaughter results when there is a death but no malice, even though the act is voluntary and the intent is to kill. The lack of malice is what separates this from a case of murder. An example of voluntary manslaughter is a killing committed in the heat of passion, with no planning and no deliberation. Involuntary manslaughter is the killing of another person through some type of negligent behavior. An example is the drunk driver who causes an accident in which another person is killed.

JUSTIFIABLE AND EXCUSABLE HOMICIDE

Another element of homicide is whether the act is considered legally justified—for instance, whether it was committed in self-defense or when otherwise permitted by law (see Table 1.1 for a state-by-state list of allowable circumstances under which citizens may use deadly force in defending themselves or their property). In such cases, the resulting death must be considered unavoidable. When confronted by an armed robber, for instance, an individual is generally considered justified in defending him- or herself with whatever amount of physical force is necessary.

Excusable homicide is the unintentional killing of another human being. There is no malice aforethought and no negligence involved in the act itself,

TABLE 1.1 State Legal Standards Defining Circumstances Under Which Citizens May Use Deadly Force

| State | Even If Life Is Not Threatened, Deadly Force May Be Justified to Protect | | Specific Crime |
	Dwelling	Property	
Alabama	Yes	No	Arson, burglary, rape, kidnapping, robbery in any degree
Alaska	Yes	No	Actual commission of a felony
Arizona	Yes	No	Arson, burglary, kidnapping, aggravated assault
Arkansas	Yes	No	Felonies as described by statute
California	Yes	No	Unlawful or forcible entry
Colorado	Yes	No	Felonies including assault, robbery, rape, arson, kidnapping
Connecticut	Yes	No	Any violent crime
Delaware	Yes	No	Felonious activity
District of Columbia	Yes	No	Felony
Florida	Yes	No	Forcible felony
Georgia	Yes	Yes	Actual commission of a forcible felony
Hawaii	Yes	Yes	Felonious property damage, burglary, robbery, etc.
Idaho	Yes	Yes	Felonious breaking and entering
Illinois	Yes	Yes	Forcible felony
Indiana	Yes	No	Unlawful entry
Iowa	Yes	Yes	Breaking and entering
Kansas	Yes	No	Breaking and entering, including attempts
Kentucky	No	No	Not specified in the statutes
Louisiana	Yes	No	Unlawful entry, including attempts
Maine	Yes	No	Criminal trespass, kidnapping, rape, arson
Maryland	No	No	Not specified in the statutes
Massachusetts	No	No	Not specified in the statutes
Michigan	Yes	No	Circumstances on a case-by-case basis

State			
Minnesota	Yes	No	Felony
Mississippi	Yes	Not specified	Felony, including attempts
Missouri	No	No	Not specified in the statutes
Montana	Yes	Yes	Any forcible felony
Nebraska	Yes	No	Unlawful entry, kidnapping, rape
Nevada	Yes	Not specified	Actual commission of a felony
New Hampshire	Yes	Not specified	Felony
New Jersey	Yes	No	Burglary, arson, robbery
New Mexico	Yes	Yes	Any felony
New York	Yes	No	Burglary, arson, kidnapping, robbery, including attempts
North Carolina	Yes	No	Intention to commit a felony
North Dakota	Yes	No	Any violent felony
Ohio	Not specified	Not specified	Felony within a dwelling
Oklahoma	Yes	No	Burglary in a dwelling, including attempts
Oregon	Yes	Not specified	Burglary or criminal trespass
Pennsylvania	Yes	Not specified	Breaking and entering
Rhode Island	Yes	Not specified	Not specified in the statute
South Carolina	No	No	Burglary, including attempts
South Dakota	Yes	Not specified	Felony
Tennessee	Yes	Not specified	Burglary, robbery, theft during the night
Texas	Yes	No	Felony
Utah	Yes	Not specified	Forcible felony
Vermont	Yes	Not specified	Not specified in the statute
Virginia	No	No	Not specified in the statute
Washington	No	No	Not specified in the statute
West Virginia	Yes	No	Any felony
Wisconsin	No	No	Not specified in the statute
Wyoming	No	No	Not specified in the statute

SOURCE: Bureau of Justice Statistics (1989), p. 31.

TABLE 1.2 Gender and Victimization of Homicide (in percentages)

Male offender/male victim	65.0
Male offender/female victim	22.3
Female offender/male victim	10.2
Female offender/female victim	2.4

NOTE: Percentages do not sum to 100 due to rounding error.

and the person must be found to have acted in a prudent and reasonable manner, as any other person in a similar situation may have acted.

In the discussion of any type of homicide, the elements of justifiable behavior, manslaughter, and degrees of homicide are always of interest, and we felt it important to introduce the issue briefly here. However, the scope of this book is limited to an overview of some particular types of homicide committed in North America, and, for the most part, our discussion will not be concerned with these other issues.

CHANCES OF BEING A MURDER VICTIM

The U.S. Department of Justice reports that the chances of being a murder victim will vary according to certain circumstances, but that most victims and perpetrators are male. This is illustrated by Table 1.2.

The data contained in Table 1.2 demonstrate the difference in gender and homicide victimization. For example, males account for 75.2% of the victims and are 3 times more likely than females to be murdered. However, this may be interpreted as good news: The rates of victimization for both males and females have reached their lowest point in more than two decades.

The offending rates for both males and females followed the same pattern as victimization rates. Thus, in 1998, males were almost nine times more likely than females to commit murder. Additionally, both male and female offenders were more likely to select male victims than female victims. But there is good news concerning homicide rates over the past several years.

TABLE 1.3 Homicide Trends in the United States, by Selected Years

Year	Homicide Rate	Estimated Number of Homicides
1950	4.6	7,020
1960	5.1	9,110
1970	7.9	16,000
1980	10.2	23,040
1990	9.4	23,400
1998	6.3	16,910

SOURCE: Bureau of Justice Statistics (2000).

Long-Term Homicide Rates

The Bureau of Justice Statistics (BJS) reports that homicide rates recently declined to levels last seen in the late 1960s (see Table 1.3). The data contained in this table show that the homicide rate was at its highest in 1980, with a rate of 10.2 per 100,000 population. It then began a gradual decline in the 1980s with little variation. It reached its lowest rate in 1998 with a rate of 6.3. Where it will go as we move into the new millennium is for the futurists in the criminal justice enterprise to foretell.

Homicide Trends by Race

Racial differences are visible when one examines the homicide rates in the United States. For example, blacks are disproportionately represented among both homicide victims and offenders. In 1998, blacks were six times more likely than whites to be murdered, and seven times more likely than whites to commit murder. The *FBI Supplementary Homicide Report, 1976-1998* states that in 1998 the white population had a victimization rate of 3.8 per 100,000 population. On the other hand, blacks had a victimization rate of 23.0. Table 1.4 illustrates the rate of victimization for both races according to selected years (Federal Bureau of Investigation [FBI], 1999).

In examining the data in this table, it is apparent that the victimization rate is falling for both whites and blacks. It peaked in 1980 and 1990, but

TABLE 1.4 Homicide Victimization Rates, by Race and Selected Years

	Rate Per 100,000 Population		
Selected Years	White	Black	Ratio of Black to White
1980	6.3	37.7	6.0
1985	5.2	27.5	5.3
1990	5.4	37.7	7.0
1995	4.8	31.6	6.6
1998	3.8	23.0	6.1

SOURCE: FBI (1999).

since 1990, it has dropped dramatically to its 23.0 number in 1998. The victimization of whites is also at an apparent all-time low during this time period.

The number of offenders is also declining. For example, in Table 1.5, it is apparent that the ratio of black killers to killers from other races is remaining relatively the same. In 1980 and 1998, this ratio was .9. In the selected years, the highest ratio was 1.0. But it must not be forgotten that even though the ratio is about the same concerning the numbers of killers and race, these data still show that blacks are overrepresented in this category per 100,000 population.

GUNS AND HOMICIDE

Homicides are committed most often with guns, especially handguns. As we examine the data reported by the FBI in Table 1.6, we see that the use of handguns in homicides peaked in the selected years.

What this information suggests is that guns play a vital role in the commission of homicide in this country. For example, since 1985, all types of guns played a role in 63% of reported murders, 45% with handguns and 18% with other types of guns (e.g., rifles, shotguns, etc.). This increased to 68% in 1995 but decreased to 65% in 1998. What is also noticeable is the drop in the percentage of murders that occurred with a knife. In 1985, for

TABLE 1.5 Number of Homicide Offenders, by Race and
Selected Years

| Selected Years | Number of Offenders | | | Ratio of Black to Other Races |
	White	Black	Other	
1980	12,275	9,767	327	0.9
1985	10,589	7,891	399	0.7
1990	11,279	11,488	400	1.0
1995	10,371	10,444	585	1.0
1998	8,357	7,908	391	0.9

SOURCE: FBI (1999).

TABLE 1.6 Weapons Used in Homicides, by Selected Years
(in percentages)

| Selected Years | Type of Weapon | | | | |
	Handgun	Other Gun	Knife	Blunt Object	Other Weapon
1980	45	18	19	5	13
1985	43	15	21	6	15
1990	50	15	17	5	13
1995	56	12	13	5	15
1998	52	13	13	5	17

SOURCE: Adapted from FBI (1999).

example, the percentage was at a high of 21%. This dropped to 13% in 1995,
where it seems to have remained. The percentage of blunt objects as murder
weapons has remained relatively stable over the past 18 years, as reported by
the FBI. What has increased is the percentage of those killed with "other

weapons." Bombs, other forms of explosives, and so on now seem to be more prevalent as weapons of fatal violence, as can be seen in the mass murder case of Timothy McVeigh.

Nevertheless, handguns account for slightly more than 50% of all murders in this country. They are the weapon of choice, and that is unlikely to change. Despite the heated debate on gun control, it is our opinion that gun control will not have a significant influence on the use of all types of guns and the commission of murder in America.

GENERAL TYPOLOGIES OF MURDERERS

Each chapter in this book discusses a certain type of homicide. Within each type of killing—partner homicide, mass murder, serial murder, and so forth—unique typologies are offered. However, before we enter into an in-depth examination of these types, we want to mention some more general types that may or may not exactly fit the typologies offered within the individual chapters.

Some killers are of the *depressive* type, and they seldom have police or criminal records. They are often under the care of mental health practitioners and are not considered psychopathic. They may believe that life is hopeless and not worth living. Such individuals are likely not only to commit suicide, but also to take loved ones with them. They view their acts of murder subjectively as acts of love. (For a more detailed analysis of the depressive personality, the reader is referred to Emile Durkheim's discussion of anomie.)

Another type of killer is the *mysoped,* or the sadistic child offender. For these individuals, murder, particularly of children, is equated with sexual gratification. Many cases of such murderers are well documented and are well known to the public. Westley Dodd killed three young boys in Washington State. Ottis Toole and Henry Lucas confessed to the murder of scores of young people (Hickey, 1997). Wayne Williams was, at one time, suspected of killing more than a dozen young children, although he was convicted of only two adult homicides (Dettlinger, 1983).

The *sexual* killer is often a serial killer. In a following chapter, we examine the sexual sadist extensively. We note here only that sexual killers connect sexual violence and murder with personal sexual gratification, and because of this, they are likely to be serial offenders (Hickey, 1997; Holmes & Holmes, 1998).

The *psychotic* killer crosses several offender types. Such people have lost contact with reality and often experience hallucinations or hear voices. For example, Joseph Kallinger, known as the "Shoemaker," heard a voice, "Charlie," that commanded that he kill everyone in the world. He started with a young neighbor; then his own son; and, finally, a nurse before being caught and sent to prison (Schreiber, 1984). He died recently in a hospital, where he had been imprisoned since his trial.

One category that encompasses many of the various types of killers discussed in this book is that of the *psychopathic* killer. Ted Bundy, John Gacy, Henry Lucas, and many other serial homicide offenders can be described as psychopathic. A psychopathic individual has a character disorder that results in his or her being unable to experience feelings of social responsibility, guilt, shame, empathy, sorrow, or any other "normal" feelings that generally result when one has harmed another person. The psychopathic killer is concerned only with his or her own feelings. To illustrate, we offer the following statement, which is part of a letter written to the first author by a psychopathic and sadistic killer currently in prison in California.

I enjoyed killing.

Yes, that's correct, I actually enjoyed killing. I enjoyed killing young females. Slender ones. Cheerleader types. The prettier the better. For me, there was no greater thrill, no greater high, and no greater meaning than that which I derived from holding in the palm of my hand the life of just such a creature, a young woman unable to resist or flee, and then slowly destroying that same life for my own personal pleasure. Ritualistic games of torture. Good old fashioned rape. Then murder. It was always quite fun. Unimaginably gratifying. Fulfilling.

Someone listening to our conversation may well find it abhorrent for me to be expressing such an apparent fondness for sadism and cold blooded murder. Some may even call it madness. Others may call it evil. Or some may call it a grotesque sickness beyond the understanding of psychiatry's most expert minds. But, regardless of the label one might wish to place upon me or my past behavior, there is no denying the fact that this deliberate snuffing out of human life was once no less than a refreshing and regular pastime for me. As natural to me as breathing air or eating food. As thoroughly satisfying as an ice cold beer on a wretchedly hot afternoon. And were I not locked away inside a prison cell this moment, there's no question about what I might otherwise be doing to occupy my hours this very same winter's night.

Perhaps even now, I might be behind a friendly smile, trading laughter with some unsuspecting stranger—a young attractive hitchhiker, or maybe a shy, unwary schoolgirl—while my brain concentrated hard on maintaining a winsome masquerade of normalcy. Even now, I might be luring such a creature into her place of doom, my guts churning with the anticipation of feeding upon terror, the misery, and the certain demise I'd soon be bringing to bear upon my hapless and captive-to-be. This very minute, I might well be strangling or beating away forever the life of yet another innocent human being—even as I did so often, so brutally, and so remorselessly throughout a long, dark chapter of my hideous past.

Obviously, I won't be killing anybody's daughter or sister this evening, and it is certain that I'll never be given the opportunity to do so again in the future. Still, it must be rather evident by now, that before I was captured and condemned to live out the rest of my life behind prison walls, I was not much different from such well-known and often psychopaths as Kenneth Bianchi, Angelo Buono, Christopher Wilder, or Ted Bundy. Like each of these men, serial killers, all of them—I, too, once roamed the streets in pursuits of human prey, luring one young woman after another to a grisly death. Like them, I killed repeatedly and without mercy, without the slightest trace of conscience. Like all of these men, I, too, was a serial killer.

Serial killer. Most people clothe their images of serial killers with only their deepest negative feelings of contempt and loathing. "Just catch the murderous bastards!" is a common refrain among society at large, "then fry their asses in the electric chair and let them rot in hell forever!" Certainly, this attitude is not a surprise, as no one knows better than I do, that a serial killer is indeed a horrifying specter, a living nightmare run amok. And, even while a serial killer actually is very much a human being—someone whose life begins just like any other life—I think it is perfectly natural that most law-abiding citizens just don't give a damn about HOW or WHY such a man should come one day to strike terror in the hearts of so many.

Understanding, then, it is extremely difficult for those who have never once entertained the idea of killing a fellow human being to consider even for a moment that NO MAN—not even one as famously heinous as a Ted Bundy—is born into this world with an inherited desire to destroy the lives of others. Yet, if a serial killer's life does indeed begin just like any other, and if he, like everyone else, leaves his mother's womb in a state of innocence, completely untouched by murderous inclinations, then isn't this evidence enough that some serial killers will continue making their deadly appearance on the American scene for as long as birthed into existence? And with this in mind, is it not pure folly to recoil away from learning all of the HOWS and WHYS behind such a person's escalation from childhood innocence to monstrous deeds of violence in adulthood?

Many years have passed since my own killing career was brought to a stop, and this prison cell wherein I now sit is literally the end of the line for me. But, while it only heightens my awareness of a desolate future to write about my past as a serial killer, I nevertheless begin this talk with you this afternoon with a sense of having no other choice but to do so. I realize few people would ever believe that I now despise what I became, or that I deeply regret the mountain of suffering and grief for which I am directly responsible. Yet, I also know that I was not the first man to haunt the streets and neighborhoods of Anytown, USA, targeting for slaughter the lives of innocent human beings—nor am I destined to be the last of my kind to do the same. And if there is to be any hope of identifying and then preventing budding, would-be serial killers from maturing into full-fledged beasts of destruction, I am convinced that this will happen only through understanding the secret inner workings of people like myself.

This serial killer has, by his own admission, killed scores of innocent people. He possesses a character defect that renders him incapable of sorrow, regret, or even wishing to stop his victimization. He stated that he does not like what he has done to others, "but don't let me out because if you do, I'll kill again and more viciously than before."

Some murderers kill because they have *organic* or *brain disorders* that make them prone to violence; that is, certain kinds of physical dysfunctions in individuals can account for their violence, whether resulting from a blow to the head or from the presence in men of an extra Y chromosome (Norris, 1988), a theory that was brought to public attention in the 1960s with the case of Richard Speck, who murdered eight student nurses in Chicago. (Actually, Speck was found not to have the extra Y chromosome, but this has not deterred Norris, who asserts that the root cause of criminality and violence lies solely in the biological realm. Despite his best efforts, this theory has not been validated.)

Some killers are *mentally retarded.* The homicides that these murderers commit often are not carried out in ways that are typical of most other killers. The mentally retarded killer will kill to cover up abnormal acts, sometimes sexual acts, sometimes accidents.

Other killers murder for reasons that have nothing to do with the various motives cited above. These are *professional hit* killers. They assassinate complete strangers for economic, political, or theological reasons.

CONCLUSION

Whatever the reason or reasons for personal violence, society may never truly understand the root cause or causes of the perpetration of personal and fatal violence. But we are of the belief that there is no single cause for the molding of the murderous personality, partly because murder is such a complex issue. There is no one single motivation for taking another person's life. The methods of killing also vary, as does victim selection. For some who kill, murder is utilitarian, the result of an impulse, or a response to a psychological need. The following chapters examine different types of murderers and their motivations.

SERIAL MURDER

Serial murder was the crime of the 1990s (Hickey, 1997; Holmes, 1990; Holmes & Holmes, 1998). Stories of serial murder have galvanized America's attention for the past 30 years (Holmes & DeBurger, 1988). The print media have fed the appetites of the public with books of both fact and fiction. For example, fact-based books are always on top of the bestseller lists. There are new books on serial killers such as *Della's Web, The A to Z*

Encyclopedia of Serial Killers, Monster, Bestial, William Heirens: His Day in Court, and two new books on Jack the Ripper: *The Mammoth Book of Jack the Ripper* and *The Belltower: The Case of Jack the Ripper Finally Solved in San Francisco.* In terms of fiction, the recently released *Hannibal,* written by Thomas Harris, immediately became the nation's bestseller in its first week of release. Other fictional bestsellers include the many works of Patricia Cornwell, such as *The Body Farm, Cause of Death,* and *Unnatural Exposure,* as well as the two works of Thomas Harris, *Red Dragon* and *Silence of the Lambs.*

These works typically examine the world of serial murder by concentrating on male serial killers, but female serial killers exist as well (see Chapter 3). Aileen Wuornos became the topic of a book titled *On a Killing Day* (Kennedy & Nolin, 1992). She is not America's first female serial killer. There have been others, many others, and they continue. For example, the week that this chapter was written, Marie Noe, age 70, was sentenced to probation for the killing of her eight children, whom she smothered to death from 1949 through 1968.

WHO IS A SERIAL KILLER?

A serial killer is a person who deliberately and with malice, kills three or more people in more than 30 days with a notable period between the murders.

Serial killers are different from mass murderers. Because they are so different, they are also difficult to understand. Serial killers such as Ted Bundy, Kenneth Bianchi, Randy Kraft, Richard Ramirez, Jeffrey Dahmer, and others strike fear in the hearts of many Americans. Can we ever truly understand the mind and mentality of those who kill sequentially? What is it about those people who kill for no apparent reason and repeat that cycle of fatal abuse? Typically, the more traditional forms of homicide involve a personal or tangential relationship between the victim and the killer. The abusive partner fatally injures a loved one. An argument outside a bar after an evening of excessive drinking turns violent. These are the types of murders that we have grown to expect and that we see almost daily in newspaper articles.

With serial murder, becoming a victim may simply be a case of being in the wrong place at the wrong time. In this scenario, the victim could be anyone, especially if the person is female or young. To the serial killer, this type of person is the most vulnerable. There is no personal confrontation in serial murder, no personal relationship. This makes serial murder all the more difficult to understand. The knowledge that many of us are vulnerable leads us not only to a shared sensation of controlled panic, but also to a growing fascination with serial murder—a dark and evil side of human behavior.

■   ■   ■   ■   ■   ■   ■   ■   ■   ■

Rafael Resendez-Ramirez:
The Railway Killer

An alert was quickly spread about a suspected serial killer who killed people alongside railway tracks in several states in the summer of 1999. The suspected killer was identified as Rafael Resendez-Ramirez.

Ramirez was not unknown to U.S. law enforcement authorities. In 1976, he was caught by the police in Brownsville, Texas, hiding on a freight train. He was quickly deported to Mexico. In less than 2 weeks, he was caught again in Michigan after changing trains in Atlanta. He was deported to Mexico again. This started his criminal career, which has included rapes, burglaries, robberies, and other crimes of violence.

The police have linked him to eight killings:

■ George Morber, and daughter Carolyn Frederick, Illinois

■ Christopher Maier, Kentucky

■ Claudia Benton, Texas

■ Noemi Dominguez, Texas

■ Josephine Konvica, Texas

■ Norman Sirnic, and wife Karen, Texas

In the near hysteria that followed the announcement of the killings by Resendez-Ramirez, citizens reported many sightings. In Louisville, Kentucky, for example, more than 100 calls came in to the Louisville Police Department that he was seen at a homeless shelter, at a McDonald's restaurant, and in an old car on the expressway, among other sightings.

Local police departments were overwhelmed with leads, too many to follow. Therefore, federal agencies, such as the FBI, DEA, and Customs, also joined in the hunt. The Texas Rangers, however, were the law enforcement agency responsible for Resendez-Ramirez's apprehension. One Ranger developed a relationship with the killer's sister, who was instrumental in getting Resendez-Ramirez to surrender to the Texas Rangers on the border of Texas and Mexico.

The agencies were all involved in a newscast. The FBI's Special Agent in Charge in Houston announced that it was an example of all agencies involved in a worthy cause, and there was room for all of the agencies to share in the apprehension of Resendez-Ramirez.

Resendez-Ramirez has been tried and found guilty.

■   ■   ■   ■   ■   ■   ■   ■   ■   ■

Serial murderers such as Ted Bundy, Angelo Buono, Douglas Clark, Wayne Williams, David Berkowitz, Kenneth Bianchi, Randy Kraft, Gary Evans, and Donald Harvey strike fear in the minds of many Americans. The recent case of Rafael Resendez-Ramirez illustrates this point perfectly. Martha Beck, Dorothea Puente, Belle Gunness, and Genene Jones are but a few of the females who have been suspected serial murderers. As noted earlier, women are seldom considered in discussions of serial offenders, although in recent years, there has been a great increase in the number of women who kill serially. These women add a dramatic and disconcerting dimension to the social problem of serial murder. One reason for this may be that women traditionally have been viewed as basically incapable of the kinds of acts attributed to serial killers.

Serial murder is difficult for the average person to comprehend, perhaps in part because of the individual risk it represents. It is hard to think of oneself as at risk of becoming a victim of such an offender. Furthermore, the damage done by the serial killer extends beyond the immediate victim to the victim's family members and friends, who suffer horribly as a result of such a crime.

SERIAL MURDER OUTSIDE THE UNITED STATES

Many people mistakenly believe that serial murder is a strictly American phenomenon (Jenkins, 1988). On the contrary, serial murder is not confined to this continent. For instance, there have been many murderers in the history of Europe who fit the operational definition of a serial killer. One of the most famous, of course, was Jack the Ripper.

In the summer of 1888, Londoners were alarmed by a series of murders of prostitutes. The news accounts of the time contained gory details of the murders, and both men and women were startled and outraged by the acts of the killer who came to be known as Jack the Ripper.

Mary Ann (Polly) Nichols is widely regarded as the Ripper's first victim, killed the night of August 31, 1888. A deep slash on her abdomen and stab wounds on her genitals suggested that the killer was left-handed. One week later, Annie Chapman became the next victim. The police found coins and brass rings at her feet, apparently laid there by her killer. She had been disemboweled so expertly that the physician who performed the autopsy said that the killer had to have some knowledge of anatomy. The next victim, Elizabeth Stride, died when her throat was cut; when police found her, she was still bleeding. Another woman, Catherine Eddowes, was killed on the same night as Stride. Her throat had been cut, and one of her kidneys had been removed, but it was not recovered at the scene. The Ripper's final victim was Mary Kelly, who was pregnant when she died. She had been disemboweled, and pieces of her flesh were suspended from the nails of picture frames on the wall next to her body. In her apartment's fireplace, police found evidence of a woman's hat and a piece of a skirt. Her body was found on November 9, 1888.

The case of Jack the Ripper has never been solved, and it still attracts the attention of those interested in serial murder. The police in England have maintained an ongoing interest in Jack the Ripper's true identity. A list of suspects has been developed, none of whom was ever arrested. The list includes the Duke of Clarence, also known as HRH Prince Albert, the heir to the British throne; James Stephen, a friend and tutor of the Duke of Clarence and son of a judge in London; and Severin Klosowski, who had had some surgical training while in Poland. Many believe that the strongest case can be made against Montague John Druitt. This young man, an athlete and a graduate of Oxford, an educated attorney who failed to practice law before the courts in England, committed suicide within weeks of the last killing.

There has also been some speculation that the killer may have been a woman, a midwife, who perhaps had some vindictive feelings toward prostitutes. This theory has no basis in investigations done by the police, especially given that witnesses stated that some of the victims had last been seen with a man who was of medium height and who wore a hat, a long coat, and spats (Noguchi, 1985; Wilson & Oden, 1987).

In Mexico City, since 1993, police report that nearly 100 women have been murdered. More liberal estimates report that the number may be as high as 200. The women, some of whom were prostitutes, many of whom were raped, were disappearing at an alarming rate. Police have arrested four men, and one informant stated that as many as eight men may have been involved in this case of serial murder involving multiple murderers.

In Vancouver, British Columbia, more than 20 female prostitutes have been murdered since 1995. In speaking with local police and the Royal Canadian Mounted Police, one author learned that there are suspicions that the killer may be a copycat (or perhaps the same killer) as the Green River Killer and a serial killer who terrorized San Diego women only a few years ago. Clearly, then, serial murder can be found all over the world.

SERIAL KILLERS IN
THE UNITED STATES

The list of serial killers in the United States reads like an unholy litany. Albert Fish, Ed Gein, Ted Bundy, Randy Kraft, David Berkowitz, John Gacy, and Jeffrey Dahmer are but a few of the notorious serial killers who have made headlines in the North American news media. Table 2.1 lists many of the known serial killers who have been active in the United States since 1900. Descriptions of the crimes of a few of these killers are offered in this section.

Albert Fish was a notable mysoped (a sadistic pedophile) in New York State in the early part of the 20th century. Thought to be responsible for the murder, mutilation, and cannibalism of scores of children, Fish was finally apprehended by the New York City Police Department for the kidnapping and murder of 10-year-old Grace Budd (Schechter, 1990).

Fish had a previous criminal record. He had been arrested several years earlier for writing obscene letters to women whose names he had secured from personal ads. He had also been arrested previously for burglary. Preoccupied with thoughts of anthropophagy (cannibalism) and coprophagia (eating excrement), Fish had been evaluated by a court-appointed psychiatrist and found to be legally sane. He was subsequently released from custody. After he was released from jail, he continued with his sexual aberrations. He urged several sexual partners to spank him as well as to urinate upon him and defecate into his mouth (Schechter, 1990).

After Fish was found guilty in the murder of Grace Budd, he was sentenced to die in the electric chair at Sing Sing. After his execution, for which he helped the guards strap him into the electric chair, an autopsy revealed that he had 29 sewing needles inserted into his penis and scrotum, something that was obviously quite sexually gratifying to him (Schechter, 1990).

Ed Gein was another bizarre serial murderer. In Plainfield, Wisconsin, Gein was known as a loner, strange and aloof to the townspeople. On the opening of deer-hunting season, Gein went into town for kerosene and a rifle. Entering the town's hardware store, he murdered the owner, Bernice Worden. The authorities quickly discovered her body hanging from a rafter in Gein's woodshed, dressed out as a slaughtered deer. They also found skulls placed on his bedposts, other skulls used as drinking cups, fingers in bowls, and a tanned, skinned face that he had used as a mask while baying at the full moon from his yard. An admitted cannibal, grave robber, and serial killer, Gein died of natural causes in a state mental hospital in 1984 (Gollmar, 1982).

Not all cases of serial murder involve such bizarre acts as those of Gein and Fish; others are more mundane. In any case, the acts of serialists— whether the unspeakable acts of Fish, Gein, John Gacy, Henry Lucas, and others, or the less bizarre murders of other killers—are perpetrated against victims who share no connection with their killers other than being unwittingly in the killers' "comfort zones," or places where the killers feel at ease to do what they wish without interference.

INCIDENCES OF SERIAL MURDER

The stories of many infamous serial killers have been told through the mass media, both electronic and print. Chris Wilder was profiled in the television movie *Easy Prey.* Ted Bundy's story was related in a TV miniseries titled *The Deliberate Stranger.* Kenneth Bianchi's story was a 2-hour program, *The Hillside Strangler.* Paperback books appear on newsstands almost weekly, telling the grisly stories: *Deranged* (about Albert Fish; Schechter, 1990); *The I-5 Killer* (about Randy Woodfield; Rule, 1988); *The Lust Killer* (about Jerome Brudos; Stack, 1983); *Nurses Who Kill* (about numerous male and female nurses who have serially murdered; Lindedecker & Burt, 1990); and *The Search for the Green River Killer* (Smith & Gullen, 1991), among others. These books contain graphic details of the murders and, in some cases, list ranges for the number of victims, from 3 to more than 50. Readers should note, however, that it would be a mistake to accept all of the data found in such books as scientific truth. There are gross errors in more than a few of these paperbacks. For example, in one new book, the author states that Lucas is serving two life sentences in Texas; Lucas is actually under a death sentence. In another book, the author talks about the John Gacy case and makes several factual errors. In the same book, the author mentions Bundy being in prison in California, rather than Florida.

The case of John Wayne Gacy is one that still lingers. For example, Gacy may have killed in other states where he worked as a building contractor. If that is true, then the 33 murders of which he was convicted will pale in comparison with the final total, which could reach as high as 100.

Even the cases reported in careful scientific research can be seriously flawed, if for no other reason than that there are untold numbers of not only victims but serial killers themselves. Our own experience bears this out. In lecturing throughout the United States on homicide in general and serial murder in particular, we are continually approached by police officers who discuss cases that they are currently investigating. More often than not, these are cases of suspected serial murder. Recently, while in Ft. Lauderdale, Florida, lecturing at a 2-week homicide investigation course, the first author spoke with an officer who was working on a serial murder case that occurred in Gainesville (five young people murdered—four young women and one man). This was only one of three cases with which this officer was involved that he believed was the work of a serial murderer. This is a typical story.

Many have attempted to estimate the number of serial killers currently murdering in North America. At one time, the U.S. Department of Justice estimated that as many as 35 serial killers were roaming the streets and towns of the United States (Reynolds, 1990). Our own research indicates that this is probably a very low estimate. Ted Bundy, in an interview with the first author conducted while Bundy was on death row in Florida, stated that it was his feeling that there were at least 100 serial murderers at large in the United States. Even this number may be too small. From our contacts with law enforcement officials all over the United States, we believe that a more accurate estimate may be as high as 200. It should be remembered that most of these killers are not involved in the murder of scores of people every year. As Bundy said in the interview, "The good [successful] serial killer will only kill two or three people a year unless he gets too greedy." A serial killer who murders too many people in too short a period of time, especially if the murders are committed in a relatively small geographic area, is more likely to be caught than is one who spaces out his murders over time and geography.

As the preceding information indicates, there is no empirically proven method for gauging the exact number of serial murderers in the United States today. The lower end of the estimate is 35, but there may be as many as 200 people who are actively killing multiple victims each year. This is a figure that will alarm many, and it may cause others to launch accusations of sensationalism. This is not our purpose, however; rather, we are concerned with educating the public as to the extent of this grave problem.

In our interviews with serial murderers already in prison, these convicts often tell us of other inmates who are in prison for rape, burglary, or other criminal acts who have admitted to our interviewees that they are serial murders. For various reasons, the serial nature of their crimes has gone un-noticed, and many of the murders they have committed have gone unsolved.

THE NUMBER OF VICTIMS

Just as it is impossible to gauge the number of serial killers accurately, it is equally impossible to give an exact number of victims who fall prey to these serialists. Bernick and Spangler (1985) estimate 5,000 victims per year, based on interviews with experts and extrapolation. However, many experts reject this number as not only inaccurate but sensationalistic.

There are hazards to judging the seriousness of serial murder simply in terms of the number of victims one serial murderer kills, or even the total number of victims of all known or suspected serial killers. In this type of homicide, as in other cases of violent crime, there are also "secondary vic-tims"—the families, friends, and acquaintances of the victims, the numbers of which are never measured (Spungen, 1998). The victimization of par-ents, spouses, and others close to the victims can continue long after the murders themselves. For example, the father of Laura Aime, one of Ted Bundy's victims, was hospitalized for depression after her murder. On one occasion, while he and Jim Massie, a Kentucky parole officer, were driving through the mountain parkway where Laura's body was found, he said, "My little baby was up there by herself, and there was nothing I could do to help her." Aime died in 1987 of heart problems, no doubt complicated by the stress of his daughter's death (J. Massie, personal communication, August 17, 1989).

A large number of serial killings [are] an attempt to silence the victims, an extreme but simple form of elimination.
—*Ted Bundy, interview, April 18, 1987*

The families and other survivors of serial murder victims are often exposed to a kind of publicity and exploitation that typically does not happen to the families of other murder victims. The mother of one serial killer's victim was so upset by a book written about the serial killer, and by what the author said about the killing of her daughter, that she was hospitalized for a week. She told James Massie that the book's author had never interviewed her about her daughter, a point about which she was quite bitter. She was additionally upset that the author had access to police information that she, as the mother of a primary victim, was denied. In an interview in which Massie spoke with both this mother and the mother of another of this killer's victims, they disapproved of a book being written concerning the murder of their daughters. One of the mothers was somewhat unnerved that an author could profit from such a crime, a fact that actually contributed to her grief as a secondary victim. She also suffered further because she heard from others what her daughter suffered before her death. She stated that she had not read the book and ended the interview by asking "Why do people write things like this?" (J. Massie, personal communication, August 17, 1989).

SPATIAL MOBILITY AND MALE SERIAL KILLERS

One of the elements used to define types of serial killers is their spatial mobility or stability. Some serial murderers move from one area to the next, killing in each area. Ted Bundy, for example, killed in a number of states, including Washington, Oregon, Idaho, Colorado, Utah, and Florida, and he is suspected of killing in California, Iowa, Pennsylvania, and Vermont. Bundy would be classified as a *geographically transient* serial murderer. These nomadic murderers kill people while they travel from one area to another. They may cruise for thousands of miles each year. Although many experts believe that nomadic serial killers drive thousands of miles because they are looking for victims, we have gathered a different picture from our interviews with convicted killers. Those with whom we have talked indicate that they never lacked for readily available victims within their own neighborhoods; their more rational explanation for their travel is that it was done to confuse police.

There are also *geographically stable* serial murderers. (It must be emphasized that the *stable* in this label has nothing to do with the personality of the killer; it refers here only to spatial mobility.) These killers do not feel comfortable leaving familiar areas when trolling for victims. Often selecting vic-

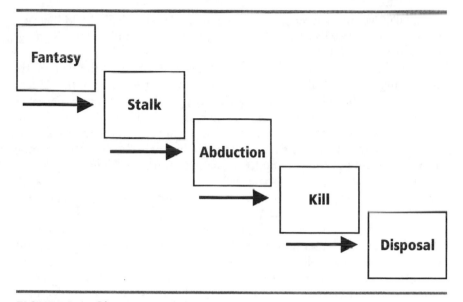

FIGURE 2.1. Phases in Serial Murder

tims close to their homes or workplaces, geographically stable serialists are more likely to be arrested than are transient killers.

PHASES IN SERIAL MURDER

Several researchers have proposed models of the phases involved in serial murder (Hickey, 1991; Norris, 1988; Rule, 1983; Stack, 1983), but there is one five-phase model that appears to be most accurate (see Figure 2.1). Not all phases of this model are present in every case; the number of phases varies, not only from one serialist to the next but, in some cases (e.g., in those committed by an organized killer), from one killing to another.

In all cases of serial killing, there is a fantasy, whether sexual, acquisitive, or demonic. This is an integral part of the killing process and is the first phase of serial murder. In other words, there must be some idea, thought pattern, or even sexual fantasy that propels the killer into the murderous process. In some cases, this fantasy is very simple, and in others, it is quite complex—but there is always a fantasy. Typically, a serial murderer's fantasy will mirror the needs, motivations, and anticipated gains of the kill. One serial killer we interviewed, for example, had a fantasy that he had incorporated as a script from a cache of pornography he found in his father's garage when he was a child.

The second phase is the stalking of the victim. As with the fantasy, the complexity of the stalk varies with time, opportunity, and the killer's compulsivity. The killer will pursue a victim according to his or her personality as well as the organization of the crime scene itself. In one case that we know of, a killer placed inexpensive watches where he knew the tires of his intended victim's husband's car would run over them, both in the driveway at her home and in the parking lot at the husband's workplace, in order to determine what time the husband left home and what time he left work. When the killer attacked the woman, he told her that he knew the window of time he had for what he wanted to do.

This stalk was complex. The stalk of the more disorganized offender, on the other hand, is typically very simple. Usually, such killers just attack suddenly, and the stalk is almost nonexistent.

More than one of the serialists we interviewed remarked that depersonalization of the victim occurs during the stalking phase. One man stated that when he started the stalk, the victim became an object; as far as he was concerned, she had no husband, no brothers or sisters, no relatives, friends, or acquaintances. While we talked, this man was holding a paper cup, which he crushed as he spoke. He said he gave no more thought to the crushing of a human life than he gave to the destruction of that cup.

The third phase in serial murder is the abduction. Not all cases of serial murder include an abduction; a disorganized offender, for example, is more likely to carry out a blitz-type attack. In an abduction by an organized offender, there may be some controlled conversation, a verbal ruse, or some other ploy that serves to move the intended victim into the killer's comfort zone for the purpose of the murder. As with other phases in the model, some abductions are very simple, and others are quite complex. Furthermore, abductions may vary with time, frequency, and the killer's feeling of compulsion.

The fourth phase is the murder of the selected victim. Holmes and DeBurger (1988) describe two types of serial murder acts: act focused and process focused. In the former type, the killing is done swiftly. The important part for this type of killer is the death of the victim; the anticipated gains for this killer are not those of sexual gratification or power. The act is decisive and immediate, and it does not depend upon a reaction from the victim. On the other hand, the process-focused killing is more typical of a lust, thrill, or power/control serialist. This person often has a mental script for the act of murder. There may be certain words to be spoken and certain acts to be performed before the murder can actually occur. Even after the death of the victim, the process-focused kill continues. For example, necrosadistic acts are quite common in this form of murder. Removal of certain parts of the body, especially sexual parts, is the rule more than the exception. The kill ends only when the killer moves into the fifth and final phase of serial murder, the disposal of the corpse.

The disposal of the body may take two forms. The killer may simply leave the site where the murder occurred, leaving the body behind. This kind of action has been linked to the *visionary* and *mission* types of serial killers (see the discussion of typology below; also see Holmes & DeBurger, 1985, 1988). The second form of body disposal happens when the killer moves the body after the murder, placing it so that it will either be found or remain hidden. When the first author asked Ted Bundy why he arranged it so that some of the bodies of his victims were found, he answered with a smile, "To let you know I'm still here" (T. Bundy, personal communication, November 17, 1987). In other words, if a serial killer disposes of a body in a location where it will be found easily and quickly, this may be seen as a form of "advertisement."

As we have noted, not all of the five phases discussed previously are part of every serial murder. However, consideration of these phases is important because of their usefulness in any investigation of a suspected serial murder case. For instance, if a victim's body has been disposed of at a location far removed from the abduction site, and if it has also been determined that the victim was murdered at yet another location, the investigator can assume that the killer is one who is closer to the organized end than to the disorganized end of the continuum. The more phases to a serial murder, the more organized the killer may be; the more organized the killer, the more truth to the traits or characteristics of the FBI's typology. For example, if an individual perpetrates a five-phase murder, it is more likely that the killer is intelligent, well educated, living with a sex partner, a police groupie, and so on. These may appear to be small points, but in a serial murder investigation, small points often become part of a synergic gestalt that leads to a successful resolution of the case.

TYPOLOGY OF MALE SERIAL MURDERERS

There have been only a few attempts to devise a typology of serial murderers based on an analysis of motivations, anticipated gains, and the analysis of the crime scene. For example, Lunde (1977) believes that most mass murderers (a type in which he includes serial murderers) are either paranoid schizophrenics or sexual sadists (Lunde, 1977). A more comprehensive endeavor is the typology offered by Holmes and DeBurger (1988). Based on interviews and the analysis of more than 400 cases of serial murder, these researchers identify four types of serial killers: visionary, mission, hedonistic, and power/control. They note that

> each type is labeled in keeping with the kinds and motives that seem to predominate in the killer's homicidal actions. Within each of these types, it is apparent that the motives function to provide the serial killer with a personal rationale or justification for the homicidal violence. (Holmes & DeBurger, 1988, p. 55)

Visionary

The visionary serial killer is impelled to murder because he has heard voices or seen visions demanding that he kill a certain person or a category of people. For some, the voice or vision is perceived to be that of a demon; for others, it may be perceived as coming from God.

JOSEPH KALLINGER— A VISIONARY SERIAL KILLER

At a young age, Joseph Kallinger first saw Charlie, a head that floated into his bedroom and commanded him to kill everyone in the world and then commit suicide. However, Kallinger waited until after he was married, with children, to begin his killings. He killed a young boy in his neighborhood; then his own son; and finally, a young student nurse. He was caught and sent to a hospital for the mentally ill in Pennsylvania.

Kallinger stated that he still saw Charlie, even after more than 30 years in prison. The head still demanded that he kill. Kallinger was not in counseling and was receiving few other mental health aids when he died of natural causes in prison.

Mission

The mission serial killer has a conscious goal in his life: to eliminate a certain, identifiable group of people. He does not hear voices or see visions. He has a self-imposed duty to rid the world of a group of people that is "undesirable" or "unworthy" to live with other human beings.

MISSION SERIAL KILLERS

Juan Chavez pleaded guilty to the strangulation murder of five men, all homosexuals. He entered his plea while serving a prison sentence for another charge. Chavez stated that he killed the gays simply because he wanted to stop the spread of AIDS in this country. He was able to avoid the death penalty in California by admitting to his crimes.

In Louisville, Kentucky, a serial killer murdered three women. He related to the police that all he was trying to do was eradicate venereal disease in this city. The women were raped and then shot to death. He was truly amazed when he discovered that the women were not prostitutes, simply women who were out late at night on their way home. This killer is presently on death row in Kentucky.

Hedonistic

The hedonistic serial killer kills simply for the thrill of it, because he enjoys it. The thrill becomes an end in itself. The lust murderer can be viewed as a subcategory of this type because of the sexual enjoyment experienced in the homicidal act. Anthropophagy, dismemberment, necrophilia, and other forms of sexual aberration are prevalent in this form of serial killing.

A HEDONISTIC SERIAL KILLER

Jerry Brudos is in Oregon State Prison for the murder of three young women, with strong evidence that there was a fourth victim. Brudos, a transvestite, had a fetish for high-heeled shoes and forced his wife and his victims to wear those shoes. He took pictures of his wife and three of the women and kept them for his own personal viewing.

With one victim, he cut off her foot and kept it in his freezer, where he would retrieve it and use it as a visual aphrodisiac. With his next victim, he cut off one breast, then with the next one, he cut off both breasts. With his last victim, he took nude pictures of her as she was hanging from her neck in his garage.

Power/Control

The power or control serial killer receives gratification from the complete control of the victim. This type of murderer experiences pleasure and excitement not from sexual acts carried out on the victim but from his belief that he has the power to do whatever he wishes to another human being who is completely helpless to stop him.

A POWER/CONTROL SERIAL KILLER

Ted Bundy killed his first victim when he was almost 16. From that time until he was apprehended in Florida, Bundy killed at least 33 young women, mostly college-aged, but also as young as 8 and as old as 26.

According to a personal interview, Ted killed in 10 states: Washington, Oregon, Utah, California, Colorado, Idaho, Iowa, Pennsylvania, Vermont, and Florida. While sexually assaulting all of his known victims, he remarked to one author (RMH) that there was no greater pleasure than to hold in one's hands the fate of another human being.

Bundy was executed in Florida's electric chair in 1989.

There are other typologies as well, some similar to Holmes and DeBurger's, and some quite different. For example, Hickey (1997) offers a similar typology but also adds a *place-specific* label to those types of serialists who murder in particular physical locations. He also includes the categories of team killers and solo killers. All three of Hickey's additional types are important to consider in the analysis of serial murder. Levin and Fox (1985) offer "murders of expediency," "murders for profit," and "family slayings."

In addition to the four types of serial murderers already mentioned, the first author has identified a fifth type, the *predator* (Holmes, 1990). This hunter of humans kills not to restore him- or herself to some type of tranquillity or state of mental peace, but simply murders continually, with no internal prohibitions to prevent it. This sexual killer has the mind-set of a predator and is on the hunt constantly. This type of serialist always has the psychological urge to victimize—not to raise himself to a psychological stance of omnipotence but more as a style of living and, for some, a form of recreation (Holmes, 1990). The first author's interviews with serialists currently in prison have revealed this type of serial killer, who seems to live to effect violence and, eventually, to kill.

TRAITS OF MALE
SERIAL MURDERERS

For an observational and empirical perspective, it is important to examine the various types of serial killers objectively. An examination of the typology offered by Holmes and DeBurger (1988) reveals the differing behavioral traits as well as motivational perspectives and perceived gains, material or psychological, of different types of male serial killers (Holmes & DeBurger, 1988). For instance, the visionary serial killer selects strangers as his victims, as do all of the types of serial murderers outlined by Holmes and DeBurger except the comfort killer. The comfort killer, in contrast, typically kills someone he knows for insurance money, business interests, or other types of material gain.

The visionary killer is involved in an act-focused killing with little planning. This killer's spatial locations appear to be concentrated. There is little inclination to move the body after the kill because once the murder is committed, the deed is done. Compare this with the traits of lust and power/control killers, who not only commit acts of necrophilia but also may keep a body long after the person is dead.

Lust, thrill, and power/control murderers are all process focused. For these types of killers, there are psychological gains to be realized from prolonging the act of the murder. This is not a part of the plan, if any plan exists, for visionary and mission killers. The mission killer also shares another trait with the visionary killer: His murders tend to be concentrated in one area, although in a wider circle than with the visionary killer.

Clearly, there are wide differences among the various types of men who are fatal serialists. These differences have important implications, not only for researchers but also for law enforcement professionals.

MOTIVATIONAL FACTORS

There are obvious differences in the motivations and anticipated gains in different serial killings. For some, the motivation may stem from a perceived demon or the voice of God. For others, it may be an intense craving found within the psyche of the killer. Some killers have described that feeling to us in interviews, even giving the sensation a name. Some call it the "beast," some the "shadow"; Ted Bundy called it the "entity" (T. Bundy, personal communication, November 17, 1987). The focus of this section is an analysis of the various factors at work in the commission of serial murder.

Basic Sources

The behavior of serial murderers is usually tied to one of three explanations. Stereotypically, serial killers are viewed as madmen or maniacs, people who may appear strange or bizarre. Although such killers may look like crazed homicidal maniacs at times, only rarely can *biogenic explanations* account for their behavior. As a rule, serial murder cannot be explained by brain waves, blows to the head received in childhood (contrary to the position taken by Norris, 1988), or defective genes in the killer. Levin and Fox (1985) are quite specific in their denunciation of this simplistic explanation. The *sociogenic approach,* which includes theories of learned behavior and cultural violence, certainly has some input into the violent personality and its propensity, perhaps, for serial murder. But sociogenic explanations cannot account directly for the etiology of the serial murderer in particular. In a study of the sexually criminal population, the FBI found that many of these criminals possess characteristics that actually are viewed as favorable to socially approved behavior ("The Men Who Murdered," 1985, p. 5). The *psychogenic approach* also fails to explain the serialist. The "typical" serial murderer is neither insane (a legal term, not a medical one) nor psychotic.

It appears that the serial murderer mind-set arises from a unique combination of traits and experiences, and that the sequence of each murderer's experiences is so unique that if it had in any way been altered, the person likely would not have become a serial murderer later in life (Holmes & DeBurger, 1985, p. 33).

Locus of Motives

What causes serial killers to murder varies not only with location but also with the frequency and duration of the motivation. For example, in an interview with the first author, Ted Bundy said that he did not kill for a period of 2 years because he was in prison. He then escaped, and within a week, he murdered in a fashion not typical of his other killings. He had previously murdered in a manner that incorporated all five phases described in Figure 2.1; however, this time, because the feeling was so strong, and the "entity" that he said made him need to kill was gnawing at his senses, he killed in an especially atypical and brutal fashion.

However, when he killed again 3 weeks after this atypical murder, he killed in a manner very similar to that of the killings he had committed before his initial incarceration. Of course, in this interview, Bundy never confessed to the killings directly; he admitted them only from a third-person perspective. It was not until shortly before he was executed that he confessed to some of his murders.

The concept of motivation is concerned with why a person behaves in a particular manner. In order to understand motivation, one must examine both the totality of the individual and the source of the motivation. For example, Joseph Kallinger, known as the Shoemaker, launched his killing career with the murder of a neighborhood youth; his own son, Joseph Jr.; and, finally, a 21-year-old nurse. The motivation for the killing came from an apparition of a disembodied head, which Kallinger called Charlie. Charlie commanded that Kallinger kill everyone in the world and then commit suicide. After his own death, Charlie promised, the Shoemaker would become a god (Schreiber, 1984). Thus, the locus of Kallinger's motivation was psychologically extrinsic. Although a valid argument can be made that Kallinger was insane and there was no Charlie, the end result is the same—the vision and voice were inside the mind of the killer, and the people in proximity to Kallinger had no knowledge of his intent.

The extrinsic motivation to kill lies outside the personality of the killer. The racially motivated "Zebra" and "Death Angel" killings are both examples of extrinsic motivation. We include paid assassins and organized crime hitmen within our definition of serial killers, although some researchers do not, and these killers' motivations also rest outside their own psyches. For such serialists, killing is simply a duty or part of their job.

The majority of serial killers' locus of motivation may be considered intrinsic. The very existence of these motives is almost always unknown to others. Even intimates of the serial murderer are seldom aware of the homicidal motives harbored in the mind of their lover, spouse, family member, or close friend. Thus, the surviving daughter of Nannie Doss, having had what she viewed as a close relationship with her mother, was shocked and astounded to learn that her mother had serially murdered 11 people, including two of the surviving daughter's siblings (Holmes & DeBurger, 1985, p. 50; Nash, 1980, p. 285).

Behavioral Orientation

It is useful to try to understand what a given killer has to gain from the commission of a particular crime. A serial killer's anticipated gains can be either material or psychological, although in our own research on scores of cases of serial murder, we have found that the preponderance of serialists kill for psychological reasons. In interviews, many have told us that the principal motivating factor in their killing was that they simply enjoyed killing. Others have stated that they were motivated by the intense feelings they got from holding the fate of other people in their hands. The more frequently such a person kills, the greater becomes his need to experience those feelings of gratification or power. The feeling becomes more than a compulsion—it becomes an addiction. And, as with most addictions, there is a need to do more and more to realize the same sense of gratification.

The accompanying sense of fantasy involved in the commission of most serial murders is further evidence that they are perpetrated for psychological gain. These fantasies often take twisted and sadistic forms:

> Much of the motive and intent in the form of fantasies are vague and loosely formulated until the murderers actually kill. With the reality of the murder, the fantasy feeds off itself and becomes more structured. As more murders are committed, the phases of the murders become more organized. (Holmes, 1989, p. 5)

CONCLUSION

Serial murder has become a serious social problem in the United States and throughout the world. With the increase in media attention as well as the perceived increase in the number of serial killers, more citizens of our country are becoming cognizant of their own personal vulnerability.

SERIAL MURDER AND THE LAW

Robert Shulman, 44, was found guilty of three murders in New York State. New York has a "serial killer" provision in the law that states that a defendant must be accused of killing three or more people within a 24-month period as part of a common scheme or plan or in a similar fashion. Shulman, a postal worker, was charged with killing three women: Kelly Bunting, Lisa Warner, and an unidentified woman.

This law, the first of its kind, is one strategy that the courts use to deal with serial killers. Will it be effective in preventing people from killing sequentially? Probably not. However, it may be society's plan to mete out "just desserts."

There is no single causative factor in the etiology of the serial killer, just as there is no single motivation or anticipated gain that is common to all serial murderers. They kill for different reasons and for different anticipated gains. Some kill for sex, some for power, some for control, and some for material gain. There are complex relationships that exist within the world of the serial killer, and professional literature has not adequately addressed the basic etiology of the serial killer.

Thus, more serious research needs to be done. There is a second generation of scholars that is accepting the task of explaining the serial killer. Perhaps there is hope for eventually understanding the mind and mentality of the serial killer.

FEMALE SERIAL KILLERS

There is some reluctance to accept women as serial killers. For example, when Aileen Wuornos was apprehended by Florida law enforcement officials, the FBI labeled her America's first female serial killer. This was simply not true. There have been many other women who have murdered sequentially. True, their numbers are not as high as men who are serial murderers, but they do exist.

Many believe that women are psychologically incapable of committing crimes as heinous and violent as those of men. Women are supposed to be the ones who mother us, not murder us. So, why do they kill?

The anticipated gains for men who are serial murderers usually rest on sexual gratification. Traditionally, it has been assumed that women do not kill for sexual reasons, nor in response to the voice of God or the growl of the devil (Holmes, 1990). They have been considered incapable of sequential fatal violence unless provoked in an abusive situation, but reality belies tradition.

It is true that most women who kill do so in response to some abusive situation (Goetting, 1987). Continued physical, sexual, and/or emotional abuse has rendered them incapable of seeing any way out of their situation other than death, the death of either their abusers or themselves. However, some women kill because they have been spurned in love, and they perceive fatal violence to be a just response.

Thus, the preponderance of women who kill do so because of ill-fated personal relationships. The typical female murderer not only kills someone she knows but also kills inside her own home (Goetting, 1989). Her methods and motivations differ fundamentally from those of the "typical" male murderer. Usually, women who kill for these reasons do not become involved in serial murder.

Some women may kill because of their involvement in cults or disciple relationships. The women in the Manson Family—Leslie Van Houten, Lynette Fromme, and others—are examples of this type. Charlene Gallego, the common-law wife of serial killer Gerald Gallego, aided in the selection and abduction of at least 10 young people (Van Hoffman, 1990). Her exact motivations are unknown; she may have been frightened into becoming an accomplice, or she may have been a willing and active participant in the killings.

KATHLEEN ANNE ATKINSON

Sometimes, a serial killer goes unnoticed for years, and sometimes, a suspected serial killer completely avoids detection. If detected and arrested, the charges may never be proved.

Atkinson, a nurse, was a suspect in the deaths of four people, two young girls and two elderly patients, in the hospital where she was a nurse in charge of the unit where the four patients died.

The police are still investigating this case of suspected serial murder.

SOURCE: www.geocities.com/Hollywood/Cinema/9301/serial/atkinson.html

Hickey (1997), who studied 34 female serial killers, found that 82% of these cases have occurred since 1900. Also, he discovered that almost half of the women had male accomplices. One of Hickey's most interesting findings is that more than one third of the women began their killing careers after 1970. He offers several explanations for this apparent increase: improved police investigations (and thus more knowledge about such cases in general), population increase, and increased media attention. The average woman killed for 9.2 years before stopping, for whatever reason. Most of the women in Hickey's sample were homemakers (32%) or nurses (18%); 15% were involved in other types of criminal careers when they became killers. One in five reported no occupation. Almost all of the women (97%) were white, and the average age was 33. One third of Hickey's sample reported having killed strangers (a much lower rate than among male serial killers), and, almost without exception, the women did not travel in their quest for victims. Most of these women killed for material gain, often using poisons or pills (see Hickey, 1997, pp. 107-118).

An increasing number of women murder multiple victims. If one uses the definition of serial murder as three or more victims over more than a 30-day period with a cooling-off period between the murders, several women can be classified as serial killers. Belle Gunness murdered an estimated 14 to 49 husbands and suitors in LaPorte, Indiana (Langlois, 1985). Nannie Doss murdered 11 husbands and family members in Oklahoma (Hickey, 1997). Martha Beck and her lover, Ray Fernandez, stalked and killed as many as 20 women.

Carol Bundy (no relation to Ted Bundy) serves as an excellent example of a suspected female serial murderer. In the early 1980s, she and Douglas Clark allegedly launched a campaign of lust murder in Los Angeles, beginning with the decapitation of Bundy's former lover, Jack Murray, and several young female runaways. She is in prison only for the murder of Murray and one female, and has admitted to these murders (Hickey, 1997); Clark is on death row in California for the murder of six young women but denies involvement in any murders (L. Farr, 1992; personal communication, 1988).

Often, women serialists kill for comfort purposes: money, insurance benefits, or business interests. Dorothea Puente of Sacramento County, California, was charged with nine murders of elderly roomers who lived in her boardinghouse. She allegedly collected and cashed the victims' Social Security checks after their murders, a scenario that has been repeated often (Blackburn, 1990).

There are, however, female serialists who kill for other than comfort reasons. Sex, revenge, and love all emerge as intrinsic motivations for homicide.

The anticipated gain and locus of motivation vary from one woman to the next, and it is this foundation of anticipated gain, locus of motivation, spatial mobility, and method of murder that serves as the basis for the following examination and categorization.

SPATIAL MOBILITY AND FEMALE SERIAL KILLERS

There is an initial distinction in serial killers based upon their geographical mobility. Geographically stable serial killers kill in or near the area in which they live. Most female serial murderers are of this type, and Carol Bundy is a good example. Bundy lived in Los Angeles and selected her victims typically from the area near the intersection of Hollywood and Vine. Killing for sexual pleasure, perhaps, and for revenge in the murder of Jack Murray, she never traveled far from her own hometown to select victims and to dispose of their bodies (Hickey, 1997).

The difference between male and female serial killers in geographical mobility may be, in part, an artifact of the traditional female role, which centers on the home and family. Additionally, women are not usually as occupationally mobile as their male counterparts, and this, too, may limit their spatial mobility. These two elements influence the victim selection process.

The geographically stable serial killer is more likely than the nomadic serial killer to be apprehended by law enforcement. This is true not only because the killer remains in the community, with personal, occupational, and social ties, but also because it means that very few law enforcement agencies are involved, so that turf issues among the investigators do not necessarily emerge as detrimental, and communication among investigators is not hampered.

Few women are transient in their killings, although there have been some. Christine Gallego is one example. She aided her common-law husband in murders in California and Nevada. The geographically transient female serial killer presents problems much like those presented by the geographically transient male killer. The mobility of the killer makes apprehension difficult, and this is complicated by turf issues and lack of communication among involved law enforcement agencies.

TYPOLOGY OF FEMALE SERIAL KILLERS

From an examination of women who have killed more than three victims in a period of more than 30 days, there emerge several types of female serialists. We call these the *visionary* killer, the *comfort* killer, the *hedonistic* killer, the *power seeker* killer, and the *disciple* killer.

The Visionary Killer

Most serial killers are not psychotic and are, indeed, in touch with reality. However, there are some who commit acts of homicide because they are psychologically, extrinsically compelled to murder. These killers may see visions that tell them to kill others, perhaps even everyone in the world.

In this type of homicide, the perpetrator has a severe break with reality. This break can be demonstrated by the person's admission that she has spoken to God, an angel, a spirit, or Satan himself. The motivation is extrinsic to the personality and comes from an apparition or an auditory hallucination. In this type of murder, attack is spontaneous. The killer selects a victim based on a description furnished by the message giver.

Martha Wise was a visionary serial killer. A 40-year-old widow living in Medina, Ohio, she killed her family members for revenge. Wise used arsenic to poison her mother after her mother ridiculed her for being involved romantically with a man younger than herself. She later fed arsenic to her aunt and uncle. She bungled an attempt to eliminate the rest of her aunt's family by administering a nonlethal amount of arsenic. Wise claimed that the devil had followed her everywhere and forced her to commit the killings (E. Hickey, personal communication, June 30, 1991).

For the visionary killer, an insanity plea can be effective, because this person is truly mentally ill. However, it must be noted that some individuals may claim to see visions or hear voices in an attempt to be found insane and thus escape severe punishment.

The Comfort Killer

Most female serial killers are of the comfort type. Their motivation is material, rather than psychological, gain, and thus the motivation is internal to the killer's psyche. There are no voices or visions from God or the devil demanding a murder.

TYPES OF FEMALE SERIAL KILLERS

Visionary: The visionary serial killer is compelled to murder because she has heard voices or seen visions demanding that she kill a certain person or a category of people. For some, the voice or vision is perceived to be that of a demon; for others, it may be perceived as coming from God.

Comfort: The comfort killer murders for money, insurance, or business interests. She kills for material, not psychological, gain. She typically kills people she knows, such as husbands, suitors, or roomers.

Hedonistic: The hedonistic serial killer is perhaps the least understood of all female serial killers. The hedonistic killer has made a vital connection between sexual gratification and fatal violence. She kills for psychological gain, typically for sexual reasons.

Power Seeker: The power seeker serial killer murders in order to attain some perceived form of power. Nurses who deliberately put their patients at risk so that they can rush in at the last moment and save them are an example of this type. Usually, nurses involved in these acts eventually tire of the charade, kill whichever patient they have been using, and move on to another.

Disciple: The disciple killer has fallen under the spell of a charismatic leader and kills upon command. Her motivation comes from outside, from the leader, and her psychological gain comes from pleasing the leader by doing his or her bidding.

The comfort serial killer typically murders people with whom she is acquainted in order to gain money—through insurance benefits, inheritance of business interests, or whatever. Such killers are not always female, of course. Before the turn of the century, one man, Herman Mudgett in Chicago, may have killed as many as 200 people for insurance and business profits (Eckert, 1985).

In 1901, Amy Archer-Gilligan opened a rest home in Connecticut. During the next 14 years, she disposed of at least 27 men and women by poison. Of the men she nursed, she married five, insured them for substantial amounts of money, and then promptly killed them. Amy also killed women after convincing them to let her assist them in rewriting their wills. She died in a mental facility in 1928 (E. Hickey, personal communication, July 12, 1991).

LYDA CATHERINE AMBROSE: A "BLACK WIDOW" SERIAL KILLER

Born in 1891, Ambrose killed five husbands, using their deaths to obtain money from insurance policies she had taken out in their names.

Like many female serial killers, she killed her victims by poison. Each husband died of "stomach problems" and "ulcers." The police eventually grew suspicious because her husbands all died soon after they married. They searched Ambrose's home and found arsenic in large amounts. The bodies of two of her husbands were exhumed, and the toxicology report revealed large amounts of arsenic in their bodies.

Ambrose was sent to prison for the murders. She escaped but was recaptured. She died of natural causes in prison.

Anna Hahn, a native of Germany, moved to Cincinnati in 1929. She volunteered to serve as a nurse for several elderly men she had met at various beer gardens. The men strangely started dying, even though Hahn "provided constant care." She called herself an "angel of mercy," but she was found guilty of several cases of murder. She was executed in May 1938 (E. Hickey, personal communication, July 12, 1991).

Janice Gibbs, a grandmother, killed her husband, three sons, and an infant grandson for $31,000 in insurance money. A native of Georgia, she was given five consecutive life sentences in 1976 (E. Hickey, personal communication, July 12, 1991).

Mary Eleanor Smith trained her son in the "art of killing," teaching him to rob men and then dump the bodies in muriatic acid beneath their home in Montana. Found guilty on multiple counts of murder, she was given a life sentence in 1920 (E. Hickey, personal communication, July 12, 1991).

Dorothea Puente, in Sacramento, California, was charged in 1988 with nine counts of murder after the authorities found bodies in the side yard of her rooming house. She allegedly killed her roomers for their Social Security checks. Earlier in her criminal career, she had been convicted of forgery in attempting to cash 34 checks belonging to tenants (E. Hickey, personal communication, July 12, 1991).

The Hedonistic Killer

Perhaps the least understood and least represented among female serial killers is the hedonistic type. Hedonism is the doctrine that pleasure is the highest good. This type of serial killer has made a vital connection between fatal violence and sexual gratification.

Carol Bundy is currently at the California Institution for Women at Frontera. She is serving consecutive sentences of 25 years to life and 27 years to life for the murder of her former lover and former manager of the apartment complex where she and Douglas Clark, the Hollywood Strip Killer, lived, as well as for the murder of a young prostitute. Bundy was allegedly involved not only in the killing of these two victims but also in the murders of several young women who were runaways and prostitutes. Clark has said that Bundy killed young women and decapitated several of them. She allegedly placed their heads in the refrigerator so that she could later retrieve them and use them in aberrant sex acts. The sexual lifestyle of Carol Bundy, which included the murder of her victims, would certainly place her in the category of the hedonistic killer. Her anticipated gain appeared to be psychological: personal and sexual pleasures. Her motivation was intrinsic to her personality, because she apparently heard no voices nor saw any visions that impelled her to murder. Bundy did not rob the victims; no money, jewelry, or personal articles were taken. It must be noted here that Bundy denies any responsibility for the murders of the young women claimed to be the victims of Bundy and Clark (Farr, 1992; Hickey, 1997). If, indeed, Bundy was intimately involved in this series of killings, she would be classed as a geographically stable, hedonistic serial murderer.

The Power Seeker

Power is the ability to influence the behavior of others in accordance with one's own desires. Power has status in any society. Women who are classified as power-seeking serial killers are those who murder as a way to attain a sense of power. The motivations and anticipated gains for these killers are very different from those of other types of female serial killers.

CHRISTINE FALLING: A POWER-SEEKING KILLER

Falling was characterized by those who knew her in her younger years as dull and slow-witted. She got married at age 14 to a man who was much older than she was. They divorced after less than 2 months. She was known to be violent and a hypochondriac, and once went to the hospital more than 50 times for snake bites, vaginal bleeding, and other treatable conditions.

The murders started with 2-year-old Cassidy Johnson. Two months later, 4-year-old Jeffrey Davis "stopped breathing," and his death was diagnosed as a heart condition. Only 3 days later, Falling killed Joseph Springs, a 2-year-old cousin of Jeffrey Davis. The next victim was an adult, William Swindle, age 77, but he was as helpless as a child. The last known victim was Falling's own 8-month-old niece. Falling had just left the doctor's office and had to return because the child had "stopped breathing."

Falling is now in prison for the murders. She received a life sentence without the possibility of parole for 25 years. Asked what she wants to do when she gets out of prison, she replied that she wanted to resume her baby-sitting job. She added that she "loves children to death."

SOURCE: "Crime: Murder by the Numbers" (1985, p. 31).

One such power-seeking female serial killer may be Jane Toppan, who was a nurse in the late 19th century. Authorities noted that two of her patients died quite mysteriously. After a series of investigations, she became a suspect in more than 100 murders. She proudly announced that she had foiled the legal authorities, "the stupid doctors," and the "ignorant relatives" for years before her discovery (Hickey, 1997). Such killers often poison their victims and then "come to the rescue," saving the victim from death's door. They are perceived by those around them as medical geniuses.

Martha Ann Johnson allegedly killed her four children, Jennyann, James, Earl, and Tibitha. Her motivation perhaps rested within the relationship she had with her husband, who had left her. Johnson, who weighed 250 pounds, said that she rolled over on top of the children in an effort to entice her husband back into the home. The ploy did not work. Although originally sentenced to death row in Georgia, her sentence was commuted on appeal.

The motivations of power-seeking female serial killers, as in the nurse example described earlier, appear to be similar to those found in people with a psychological condition called Munchausen Syndrome by Proxy, which has received increasing media attention. Those who have this illness, usually mothers, have been known to fabricate and/or induce medical problems in their children. Apparently, power-seeking serial killers are motivated by their own self-perceptions of worthlessness to create life-and-death situations in which they can be heroes and thus gain feelings of importance.

The motivation of the power seeker is clearly intrinsic. Satisfaction for this killer does not come from the act of killing itself but from being perceived as the one responsible for averting a death. The rewards come in the form of adulation from others on the scene as well as from relatives of the patient who almost died.

The Disciple Killer

Some women kill because they are under the influence of a charismatic leader, the most infamous of whom is Charles Manson. Lynette Fromme, Leslie Van Houten, and the other women in the Manson Family committed unspeakable acts of violence because they wanted to please Manson.

The motivation for this type of female serial murderer is linked to a source outside the psyche: the charismatic leader. Jim Jones is another example of such a leader. Despite various problems in his final days, including financial difficulties and illness, Jones was able to influence many of his followers to do whatever he wished, up to and including suicide. The gain for the disciple killer is psychological: She hopes to be accepted by her idol.

MUNCHAUSEN SYNDROME BY PROXY

Jennifer Bush had been chronically ill for most of her young life. Plagued by complex intestinal problems, she had been shuttled from doctor to doctor by her mother, Kathleen Bush, in the hope of finally finding an answer to what ailed her.

Jennifer's problems were so severe that by the time she was 7 years old, she had been hospitalized nearly 200 times and had had 40 operations, including the removal of her gallbladder, appendix, and much of her intestines. Her medical bills had already topped $2 million, which exhausted her family's health benefits.

Through it all, Kathleen Bush, a home health care clerk, remained the supportive, devoted mother—that is, until authorities arrested her in 1996, accusing Kathleen of deliberately causing Jennifer's medical problems by giving her unprescribed drugs, tampering with those that were prescribed, and contaminating the feeding tube in her stomach with fecal bacteria.

The nurses at the medical center where Jennifer stayed had become suspicious at least 4 years earlier, when they noticed that her condition deteriorated rapidly whenever her mother was around. However, state officials were unable to prove any kind of abuse at that time. But in 1996, after an anonymous complaint, they reopened the investigation and filed a formal complaint against Kathleen. Jennifer's medical records were reviewed by a noted Munchausen expert at Boston's Children's Hospital, who concluded that this was, indeed, a clear case of Munchausen Syndrome by Proxy.

Jennifer was immediately removed from her parents' home and placed in foster care. Her health began to improve steadily, and as of this writing, she is a healthy, active teenager. Kathleen Bush was convicted in 1999 of aggravated child abuse and organized fraud and sentenced to 5 years in prison. Her case is currently on appeal

Victim selection is typically arranged by the leader. For example, Manson allegedly selected the homes to which he sent his disciple killers.

Although the Manson Family murders are perhaps the most famous example of the disciple killer, there have been other cases as well. In 1982, Judy Neelley and her much older husband, Alvin, were involved in forgeries, burglaries, and robberies. The couple eventually began to abduct, abuse, rape, and murder their victims. Judy claimed that she was completely dominated by her husband, and that he forced her to commit torture and murder. While in Alabama, they abducted a 13-year-old girl and held her captive for several days. Judy watched while Alvin raped the girl on four occasions and while he tortured and abused the child. Finally, Judy injected liquid drain cleaner into the girl's veins, but when that failed to kill her, Judy shot the girl in the back and pushed her over a cliff.

The Neelleys later abducted a husband and wife. They marched the couple into a wooded area and shot them both. The man survived the shooting and later testified against the Neelleys. They were arrested, tried, and convicted. Alvin is now serving a life term in Georgia; Judy was sent to death row in Alabama, but her sentence was recently commuted to life imprisonment. The final number of actual victims is unknown (E. Hickey, personal communication, July 28, 1991).

Charlene Gallego married her husband, Gerald, unaware that he was still married to another. Unlike her husband, Charlene grew up in a home where love and affection were shown freely. Soon after her involvement with Gerald began, however, she accepted his lifestyle, including his bizarre sexual fantasies. She solicited young women for Gerald by promising them employment and then drove them around in a van while Gerald raped them. She then drove to the places where Gerald would kill them and dispose of their bodies. Involved in the killings of at least nine young women and one young man, Charlene finally turned state's evidence and served 16 years in prison in Nevada (Blackburn, 1990). She was released in 1997.

Martha Beck and her lover, Ray Fernandez, advertised in "lonely hearts" magazines for female companionship. The women who answered these ads quickly became victims. They were strangled, battered, drowned, poisoned, or shot to death. To demonstrate her affection for her lover, after drowning a 2-year-old child in a bathtub, while her hands still held the dead girl under water, Beck summoned Fernandez, gleefully exclaiming, "Oh, come and look what I've done, sweetheart." A reliable estimate of the number of women killed by Beck and Fernandez is 20. Arrested in Michigan and sent to New York to stand trial for murders committed there, both were electrocuted in Sing Sing in 1951 (E. Hickey, personal communication, July 17, 1991).

A strange personal chemistry appears to exist in some relationships that results in a series of murders that probably would not have occurred had the two parties not met. In the case of Carol Bundy and Douglas Clark, neither had killed before they shared their common fantasy. This was also true for Angelo Buono and Kenneth Bianchi, the Hillside Stranglers, and for Alton Coleman and Debra Brown. Brown lived with the abusive Coleman; violence became a part of their relationship, and savagery became an integral part of their killings. Brown followed Coleman's lead when she killed an elderly couple in Cincinnati using a four-foot wooden candlestick, a crowbar, vise-grip pliers, and a knife. She is thought to have killed as many as eight people in the company of Coleman. She received two death sentences, life in prison, and a dozen additional years. Even after her trial and incarceration, Brown remained loyal to her lover and signed legal documents making the two common-law partners (Hickey, 1991, pp. 179-180).

TRAITS OF TYPES OF FEMALE SERIAL KILLERS

The distinctions among the types of female serial killers discussed earlier may be refined and categorized into definitive traits. Knowledge about these traits can lead to better understanding and increased apprehension of female serial killers. The behavioral traits of different kinds of female serial killers are discussed in this section. This examination centers on victim selection, methods, and spatial locations of murders. Table 3.1 shows these factors and how they apply for each of the five types of female serial killers developed in this chapter. For example, the visionary serial killer typically attacks nonspecific victims; they are chosen randomly and are usually strangers. Among women serialists, only comfort murderers typically kill people they know—husbands, suitors, children, and so on. Disciple killers murder victims preselected by their leaders and thus are not involved in determining their victims' suitability for assault.

Motives for murder also vary with the type of female serialist. For instance, only the visionary killer kills spontaneously. Comfort murderers are act-focused killers; they kill because of anticipated material gain, and the process of killing is not the important part. Hedonistic killers, on the other hand, are process focused—they kill for the pleasure they get out of the killing itself. The crime scene of the visionary killer is typically disorganized, whereas the crime scenes of the other types of killers are organized. Finally,

TABLE 3.1 Homicidal Behavioral Patterns of Female Serial Killers

Factors	Visionary	Comfort	Hedonistic	Disciple	Power
Victim selection					
Specific		X	X		X
Nonspecific	X			X	
Random	X		X		
Nonrandom		X		X	X
Affiliative		X			
Strangers	X		X	X	X
Methods					
Act focused	X			X	X
Process focused		X	X		
Planned		X	X	X	X
Spontaneous	X				
Organized		X	X	X	X
Disorganized	X				
Spatial locations					
Concentrated	X	X			
Nomadic			X	X	X

hedonistic and power-seeking killers usually dispose of the bodies of their victims somewhere distant from the places where the crimes occurred.

The spatial mobility of female serial killers varies as well. For example, visionary and comfort types tend to kill within the areas in which they live. The other three types are more nomadic in their crimes, not unlike the lust, thrill, and power/control types among male serial murderers (Holmes & Holmes, 1998).

CONCLUSION

Serial murder is a social problem that certainly affects the criminal justice system. Until recently, many of those both inside and outside the criminal justice system thought that serial killing was confined only to male offenders. Research on the perpetration of such crimes as sequential homicide has proved that this is not the case. There seems to be an increasing number of women who are turning to violent crimes to satisfy their needs, but whether this is biologically or sociologically based is still debatable. Dabbs and Hargrove (1997), for example, believe that women who are violent possess a higher level of testosterone than do their sisters who are not criminals. They also add that the women in prison whom they tested and who were found to have high levels of testosterone were more aggressive and dominating. Women with low testosterone levels were more apt to be "sneaky and treacherous" (Dabbs & Hargrove, 1997). Regardless of this information, the debate will continue.

Women still represent only a very small percentage of all cases of serial murder, but this does not negate the potential danger such women pose to society. The character of the female serial killer is also changing. As Hickey (1991) notes, "Over the past few years, female offenders killed fewer family members . . . while increasingly targeting strangers. . . . Those who had male partners were much more likely to use violence in killing their victims" (p. 127).

Clearly, no single motivation can account for the murderous acts of female serial killers. Money, sex, and revenge are all motives, but the exact etiology is unknown. Regardless, the peril will continue.

MASS MURDER

There is a great deal of misunderstanding about what is meant by the term *mass murder*. Often the terms *mass murder, serial murder,* and *spree murder* are used interchangeably, even though there are fundamental differences among these three forms of multicide (i.e., the killing of three or more victims). Each of these three types of murder involves unique motivations, anticipated gains, methods of victim selection, methods of killing, and other important elements.

This chapter examines only one form of multicide, mass murder. Within this type of murder, some elements will differ. For example, the weapon used may be a gun, arson, or a bomb smuggled aboard an airplane. The anticipated gains of mass murderers may vary also. This chapter explores the nature of mass murder in depth and points out the ways in which it is distinct from serial and spree murder.

WHAT IS MASS MURDER?

Simply stated, mass murder is the killing of a number of people at one time and in one place. Obviously, however, there is more to mass murder than this simple definition. It is immediately apparent that there are elements that separate mass murder from other forms of homicide.

The preceding definition is a useful starting point for differentiating mass murder from other forms of murder. One issue to be decided is how many people are considered "a number." How many people need to die for a mass murder to have taken place? Holmes and DeBurger (1985, 1988) and Hickey (1991) suggest that three is the appropriate number. Other researchers, such as Hazelwood and Douglas (1980), believe that four deaths should be the criterion. Dietz (1986) offers the number of three "if we define mass murder as the willful injuring of five or more persons of whom three of more are killed by a single offender in a single incident" (p. 480).

Dietz's definition is cumbersome, especially because it adds the element of injured victims to the basic definition. Of course, if only 2 people are killed and 30 are saved through heroic actions taken by medical personnel, would this not be a mass murder situation? Such are the games played by anyone who tries to use only a base number as an integral part of a definition. We prefer to consider three the critical number, without consideration of others who may be injured and would have died if not for successful emergency medical care. The critical concern in the definition is the number of people murdered.

Time and place are two further elements in the basic definition of mass murder. Our definition specifies that the murders must occur "at one time and in one place." Typically, the act of mass murder is carried out in a single, episodic act of violence. An example is the 1984 incident that took place at a McDonald's restaurant in San Ysidro, California. The victims, 40 in all (21 died), just happened to be together in one place—the restaurant—and the killings all occurred over a very short time span. However, it is prudent to recognize that mass murders may be carried out over a longer period—minutes or even a few hours—and also at more than one geographic location—perhaps only a few blocks apart. For example, a mass killer may go into one business establishment and kill several customers, and then go across town and kill another person. This may be considered an act of mass murder despite the fact that it did not occur strictly at one time and in one place.

These components illustrate the important differences among mass murder, serial murder, and spree murder. Serial murder is defined as the killing of three or more people with more than a 30-day period between the first and last kills. Spree murder is the killing of three or more people usually within a 30-day period. With spree murder, there is typically an accompanying felony, such as robbery. Determining the form of multicide is the first step toward a successful resolution of the case; this determination holds the key to understanding the character of the person who would commit such an act.

Other Significant Differences

One additional difference between mass murder and serial murder is that mass murderers often die at the scenes of their crimes, either by committing suicide or by forcing the police to take lethal action. In only a few cases do they turn themselves in to the police. Serial killers, on the other hand, take great pains to avoid detection and apprehension (Hickey, 1997; Holmes & DeBurger, 1988; Holmes & Holmes, 1998).

Another difference between mass murder and serial murder can be found in the different responses each provokes within the community. Typically, when a mass murder takes place, the immediate community, as well as the rest of the nation, is informed, and expressions of alarm at the slaughter of innocent victims follow quickly. The impact is immediate. The panic in the community is direct and severe, but short-lived. This is not the case with serial murder, which can disrupt community life for long periods. In Seattle, for example, residents have been terrorized for more than 15 years in the wake of the murders of more than 40 young women, some prostitutes, some not. In one large midwestern city, more than 40 unsolved homicides have instilled fear in the community. Unlike in cases of mass murder, there is no perceived end when serial murders occur.

The perpetrators of mass murder and serial murder are also very different. The mass murderer is often perceived to be a demented, mentally ill person. People interviewed on television about a mass murderer often say that the killer had been seeing a mental health professional, had been on medication, had been threatening fellow employees, and so on. More research may show an early pattern that may be predictive of a mass murderer personality;

thus far, however, this has not been researched adequately (Dietz, 1986; Hickey, 1997; Norris, 1988). It often seems that if only we had the expertise and the resources, we would be able to detect such people before they kill. But this is not the case with the serial murderer. Ted Bundy, Gerald Stano, Randy Kraft, and others like them were all people who were not easily discernible as dangerous. They walked into the lives of many, often invited, and dispatched them with little concern. Such cases can cause great social paranoia, because individuals perceive themselves to be personally vulnerable. Episodes of mass murder do not seem to inspire this same sense of fear and anxiety.

INCIDENTS OF MASS MURDER

Mass murder is neither a strictly American nor a modern phenomenon; such cases are spread across history and have taken place all over the world. In recent times, it seems that mass murder has increased, but it is unclear whether the incidence of mass murder has actually risen or whether we are now simply better able to detect and thus report it. Some specific modern cases of mass murder are described below. Table 4.1 presents a list of mass murders dating from 1949 to 1989, and Table 4.2 shows the increased incidence of mass murder since 1990.

In July 1966, Richard Speck entered a Chicago apartment occupied by nine student nurses. Methodically, brutally, and coldly, Speck led eight of the young women, one at a time, into a room and then sexually assaulted and murdered them. Thinking that he had killed all of the young women in the apartment, and losing count that there were truly nine, he calmly walked out the front door and disappeared. The one survivor, however, had hidden under a bed, and after Speck left, she screamed hysterically until help arrived. Speck was captured almost immediately by the Chicago police. He was tried and convicted, and he received multiple life sentences. Escaping the death penalty, he died in an Illinois prison in 1991.

Charles Whitman, another mass murderer, confessed to his college counselor that he had an overwhelming urge to kill people. The counselor, not sensing the immediacy of Whitman's condition, scheduled an appointment for him the next day. After leaving the office, Whitman went to his mother's home and killed her. He then arrived at his own apartment and killed his young wife. The next day, Whitman climbed to the top of a tower on the campus of the University of Texas at Austin and, for 96 minutes, shot indiscriminately at passersby. He shot 46 people, of whom 16 died. Whitman was finally shot and killed by a police officer. The medical

(text continues on page 66)

TABLE 4.1 Mass Murderers or Suspected Mass Killers Pre-1990

Year	State	Murderer (or Suspected Murderer)[a]	Death Toll
1949	New Jersey	Howard Unruh	Shot 13 neighbors
1950	Texas	William Cook	Shot 5 family members
1955	Colorado	John Graham	Bomb on plane, 44 died
1959	Kansas	Richard Hickock	Stabbed/shot 4 members of Culter family
1966	Illinois	Richard Speck	Stabbed/strangled 8 student nurses
1966	Texas	Charles Whitman	Shot 16, mostly students
1966	Arizona	Robert Smith	Shot 5 women in beauty saloon
1969	California	Charles Watson	Stabbed 7 people for Charles Manson
1969	California	Patricia Krenwinkel	Stabbed 7 people for Charles Manson
1969	California	Linda Kasabian	Stabbed 7 people for Charles Manson
1969	California	Susan Atkins	Stabbed 7 people for Charles Manson
1970	North Carolina	Jeffrey MacDonald	Stabbed 3 family members
1971	New Jersey	John List	Shot 5 family members
1973	Georgia	Carl Issacs	Shot 5 members of a family
1973	Georgia	Billy Issacs	Shot 5 members of a family
1974	Louisiana	Mark Essex	Shot 9, mostly police officers
1974	New York	Ronald DeFeo	Shot 6 family members
1975	Florida	Bill Zielger	Shot 4 adults in a store
1975	Ohio	James Ruppert	Shot 11 family members
1976	California	Edward Allaway	Shot 7 coworkers

(continued)

TABLE 4.1 Continued

Year	State	Murderer (or Suspected Murderer)[a]	Death Toll
1977	New York	Frederick Cowan	Shot 6 coworkers
1978	Guyana	Jim Jones	Poisoned/shot 912 cult members
1980	Georgia	Wayne Coleman	Shot and beat 6 people
1982	Pennsylvania	George Banks	Shot 13 family members and acquaintances
1983	Louisiana	Michael Perry	Shot 5 family members
1983	Washington	Willie Mak	Shot 13 people in head
1983	Washington	Benjamin Ng	Shot 13 people in head
1984	California	James Huberty	Shot 21 people at McDonald's
1985	Pennsylvania	Sylvia Seigrist	Shot several people at mall, 2 died
1986	Oklahoma	Patrick Sherrill	Shot 14 coworkers
1986	Arkansas	Ronald Simmons	Shot 16 family members
1987	Florida	William Cruse	Shot 6 people at mall
1988	Minnesota	David Brown	Killed 4 family members with axe
1988	California	Richard Farley	Shot 7 people in a computer store
1988	California	Patrick Purdy	Shot 5 children in a school playground
1988	North Carolina	Michael Hayes	Shot 4 neighbors
1989	Kentucky	Joseph Wesbecker	Shot 8 coworkers

a. In some cases, the person named here may not have been charged with all of the victims shown in the death toll because of the expense of further trials or lack of direct evidence to ensure conviction. In some cases, for example, a person may be charged with only one murder even though the police and the courts believe he or she is responsible for more.

TABLE 4.2 Mass Murderers or Suspected Mass Murderers in the Modern Era, 1990-Present

State	Murderer (or Suspected Murderer)[a]	Death Toll
Alabama	Jason Williams	Shot 3 family members and 1 other adult
	Joseph Akin	Allegedly killed 18 patients in a hospital
Alaska	Paul Ely, Jr.	Killed his wife and 2 children
	James Price	Killed 3 boarding house residents
Arizona	Shane Harrison	Killed 5 people in a robbery
	Norman Yazzie	Shot his 4 children
	Robert Smith	Killed 5 people in a beauty college
Arkansas	Mitchell Johnson	Killed 4 fellow students and a teacher
	Andrew Golden	Killed 4 fellow students and a teacher
	Damien Echols	Killed 3 young boys
	Jason Baldwin	Killed 3 young boys
	Jesse Misskelley	Killed 3 young boys
California	Frederick Davidson	Killed 3 members of his thesis committee
	Eric Houston	Killed 4 people at his former high school
	Arturo Suarez	Killed 4 people
	Sandi Nieves	Killed 4 children
	John Orr	Killed 4 people by arson
	Susan Eubanks	Killed her 4 children and then herself
	Michael Perry	Killed 5 people, including his parents
	Joshua Jenkins	Killed 5 family members
	Jorjik Avanesian	Killed 7 family members

(continued)

TABLE 4.2 Continued

State	Murderer (or Suspected Murderer)[a]	Death Toll
	Gian Ferri	Killed 6 in an attorney's office
	Leonardo Morita	Killed his wife, 3 children, and maid
	Willie Woods	Shot 4 fellow workers
	Alan Winterbourne	Shot 5 people
	Dora Buenrostro	Killed her 3 children
	Christopher Green	Killed 4 at a post office
	Ronald Taylor	Killed 5 friends and relatives
Colorado	Eric Harris	Killed 13 at his high school
	Dylan Klebold	Killed 13 at his high school
	William Neal	Killed 3 women with an axe
	Albert Petrosky	Killed his wife, 1 shopper, and a police officer
Connecticut	Geoff Ferguson	Shot 5 people
	Errol Dehaney	Killed his wife and 2 children
	Matthew Beck	Killed 4 coworkers
Delaware	Richard Herr	Killed 3 fellow workers
Florida	James Pough	Shot 13 in an auto loan company
	Henry Carr	Killed 2 police officers and a young boy
	Miranda Shaw	Set fire to her 3 children and herself
	Curtis Windom	Shot his girlfriend and 2 adults
	Clifton McCree	Shot 5 coworkers
	David Vitaver	Killed his wife, son, and daughter
	Carl Brown	Shot 8 people in a machine shop

Georgia	Scott Heidler	Killed his foster parents and 2 children
Hawaii	Orlando Ganal	Shot 4 people, including his in-laws
	Bryan Uyesugi	Killed 7 fellow employees
Illinois	Lavern Ward	Killed his girlfriend and their 2 children
	Charles Smith	Killed his girlfriend and her 3 relatives
	Eric Matthews	Killed his wife, 2 ex-girlfriends, and his stepson
Indiana	John Stephenson	Shot 3 people
	Joseph Corcoran	Killed 6 people, including his brother
	John Ritzert	Shot his 3 children
Iowa	Gang Lu	Shot 5 college officials and college students
	Larry Buttz	Killed his wife and 2 children, and then killed himself
Kentucky	Michael Brunner	Shot his girlfriend and her 2 children
	Robert Daigneau	Shot his wife and 3 strangers
	John Stephenson	Shot a husband, wife, and another man
	Michael Carneal	Killed 3 fellow students
	Jason Bryant	Killed 3 members of a family
	Natasha Cornett	Killed 3 members of a family
	Crystal Sturgill	Killed 3 members of a family
	Karen Howell	Killed 3 members of a family
	Dean Mullins	Killed 3 members of a family
	Joe Risner	Killed 3 members of a family
	Ronnie Sparks	Killed 3 backpackers
	Clay Shrout	Killed his father, mother, and 2 sisters
Louisiana	Antoinette Franks	Killed 4 patrons in a restaurant and a police officer
	Michael Fisher	Stabbed his mother, stepfather, and stepbrother
	Michael Perry	Killed 5 family members

(continued)

TABLE 4.2 Continued

State	Murderer (or Suspected Murderer)[a]	Death Toll
Maryland	Mark Clark	Bombed his wife and 4 children
	Bruman Alvarez	Killed a doctor, his 3 daughters, and a housepainter
Massachusetts	Anthony Clemente	Killed 4 family members
	Damian Clemente	Killed 4 family members
	Peter Contos	Killed his girlfriend and their 2 children
	Mark Clark	Bombed his wife and 3 children
	Timothy Prink	Killed 4 family members
Michigan	Lawrence DeLisle	Drowned his 4 children
	Ilene Russell	Set a fire that killed 4 adults and 1 child
	Thomas McIvane	Shot 3 children
	Allen Griffin, Jr.	Shot 3 people at a bank
Minnesota	Paul Crawford	Shot 4 neighbors
	Khoua Her	Strangled her 6 children
	David Brown	Killed 4 family members
	James Schnick	Killed 7 family members
Mississippi	Ken Jones	Killed his wife and 4 coworkers
	Kenneth Tornes	Killed his wife and 4 coworkers
	Luke Wooodham	Killed his mother and 2 students at a high school
Missouri	James Johnson	Killed 4 people
	Bruman Alvarez	Stabbed 5 people to death
	Mark Christeson	Killed a mother and 2 children
	Jesse Carter	Killed a mother and 2 children
	Jeffrey Sloan	Killed his parents and 2 brothers

Montana	Reginald Sublett	Killed his ex-girlfriend, their son, and 2 others
Nebraska	Marvin Nissen	Killed 3 women
	John Cotter	Killed 3 women
Nevada	Martin Garcia	Killed 2 stepdaughters and niece
New Hampshire	James Colbert	Strangled his wife, suffocated 3 daughters
	Carl Drega	Killed 4 people in his town
New Jersey	Joseph Harris	Shot 4 people in a post office
New Mexico	Stanley Secatero	Killed 4 relatives on a reservation
New York	Julio Gonzalez	Set a fire in a nightclub that killed 87 people
	Andrew Brooks	Shot his father and 3 men
	Colin Ferguson	Shot 6 people in a subway
	Michael Vernon	Killed 5 people in a shoe store
	Patrick Biller	Killed his wife and 3 children
	Roland Smith	Burned 7 people to death
	Michael Stevens	Killed girlfriend's mother, sister, and stepfather
	Gary Evans	Killed 5 people
	Richard Timmons	Killed his wife and 2 children
North Carolina	James Davis	Killed 3 coworkers
	Jose Osorio	Killed 5 migrant workers
	Alonzo Osorio	Killer 5 migrant workers
Ohio	Kim Chandler	Shot her 3 children
	Joseph Lundgren	Shot 5 family members of a cult
	Richard Brand	Shot 5 family members of a cult
	Todd Hall	Killed 9 people in a fireworks store
	Gerald Clemons	Killed 3 people at his former workplace

(continued)

63

TABLE 4.2 Continued

State	Murderer (or Suspected Murderer)[a]	Death Toll
Oklahoma	Timothy McVeigh	Killed 168 people in the federal building
	Terry Nichols	Killed 168 people in the federal building
	Danny Hooks	Killed 5 women in a crack house
Oregon	Girley Crum	Killed 3 adults and 2 children
	Ray DeFord	Killed 8 people by arson
	Kipland Kinkel	Killed his parents and students at his school
	David Whitson	Killed his wife and 3 children
Pennsylvania	David Freeman	Stabbed and beat to death his parents and brother
	Bryan Freeman	Stabbed and beat to death his parents and brother
	George Banks	Killed 9 family members
	Miguelina Estevez	Killed her 3 children and herself
	Robert Renninger	Killed his wife and 2 children
South Carolina	Fred Kornahrens	Killed his wife, her father, and his 2 children
	John Satterwhite	Killed his son and 3 stepchildren
Tennessee	Courtney Matthews	Shot 4 people in a Taco Bell
	David Housler	Shot 4 people in a Taco Bell
	Tony Carruthers	Killed 3 people
	James Montgomery	Killed 3 people
	Jason Bryant	Killed 3 members of a family
	Karen Hoill	Killed 3 members of a family
	Daryl Holton	Killed his ex-wife and 3 children
	Everett Cobb	Killed his ex-wife, her new husband, and a friend

Texas	George Hennard	Shot 22 people in a restaurant
	James Mankins	Killed 5 people at a restaurant
	James Simpson	Killed his wife, boss, and 3 coworkers
	Steven Renfro	Killed his girlfriend, aunt, and neighbor
	Robert Coulson	Killed his adopted parents and 3 others
	Coy Wesbrook	Killed his wife and 3 others
	Virgil Martinez	Killed his wife, 2 children, and a friend
Vermont	Richard Stevens	Killed 3 people near a college campus
Virginia	Douglas Buchanan	Killed his father, stepmother, and 2 stepbrothers
Washington	Timothy Black III	Shot 3 women and unborn fetus
	Barry Loukaitas	Killed teacher and 2 fellow students
	Martin Pang	Killed 4 firefighters
	Alex Barany Jr.	Killed a husband, wife, and their 2 children
	David Anderson	Killed a husband, wife, and their 2 children
	Sam Lau	Killed his wife and 2 children
West Virginia	Ricky Brown	Killed 5 children
	Barbara Brown	Killed 5 children
	Janette Abler	Killed 5 children

a. In some cases, the person named here may not have been charged with all of the victims shown in the death toll because of the expense of further trials or lack of direct evidence to ensure conviction. In some cases, for example, a person may be charged with only one murder even though the police and the courts believe he or she is responsible for more. Also, a few of the people listed here have not yet gone to trial.

examination searched for a biological explanation for his condition. Doctors examined his brain for a tumor, hoping to find one that would explain Whitman's violent behavior, but no conclusive medical evidence was found (Hickey, 1991, p. 4).

Joseph Wesbecker was on disability leave from his job with Standard Gravure, a printing company in Louisville, Kentucky, when he entered the company building in September 1990 looking for supervisors. A mental patient still in therapy and under medication for periods of depression, he had mentioned previously to several coworkers that someday he would kill his bosses (Scanlon & Wolfson, 1989). Carrying a bag under one arm that contained several assault weapons as well as ammunition, he got off an elevator and immediately fatally wounded three people (one a female friend of the first author), and then shot four more fellow employees before he finally killed himself.

In the late 1980s, in Stockton, California, Patrick Purdy drove to the Cleveland Elementary School playground, got out of his car with a gun, set the car on fire, and then walked to the side of the playground and opened fire on children playing there. After killing five children, he killed himself (Caputo, 1989; "Death on the Playground," 1989; "Slaughter in a School Yard," 1989).

Perhaps one of the most infamous cases of mass murder is that of James Oliver Huberty. A skilled worker for the Babcock and Wilcox Company in Massilon, Ohio, Huberty was laid off from his job as a welder because of deteriorating economic conditions in northeast Ohio at the time. Moving to California, Huberty and his wife and two daughters settled in a working-class neighborhood. Gaining employment as a security officer, a job for which he was overqualified, he soon found himself unemployed again. According to an interview Mrs. Huberty later gave, the morning of July 18, 1984, started off quietly enough (Home Box Office, 1988). The family went to the San Diego Zoo and later stopped for lunch at a McDonald's restaurant a half block from the Huberty apartment. After a lunch of Chicken McNuggets, fries, and a Coke, Huberty left the restaurant with his family. Mrs. Huberty stated that she was tired from the morning excursion to the zoo and had plans to go to the local grocery store later for food for dinner. She decided to take an afternoon nap first. While she was lying down in the bedroom, her husband came in and told her he was "going to hunt humans." He often said things to get her upset, and this time, she decided that whatever he said, it was not going to bother her. He kissed her good-bye, armed himself with weapons he kept in the apartment, walked out the front door, and turned right. Walking into McDonald's, he started firing, shooting 40 people and killing 21. Huberty was eventually killed by a police sharpshooter from a building across the street.

What kind of a man would walk into a fast-food restaurant and shoot innocent people? An angry man. A disenfranchised man. A man who believed that the world had done him a great disservice. Huberty perhaps reflected back on his life and saw failure after failure. There was evidence of his rage in his past behavior. In his home in Ohio, Huberty practiced shooting his gun into the basement wall. He kept a cache of weapons, and on more than one occasion, he pointed a rifle at his neighbors from his back yard. He never fired, but nevertheless, he frightened his neighbors continually. Forced to leave a job in Ohio after 15 years of faithful service, losing several homes and apartment houses in Ohio, he migrated to California only to lose a job there. Huberty fought back at a society he believed had treated him unjustly. But why did he murder innocent people, strangers? Clearly, they were not responsible for his problems. Maybe they represented something to him that he was not: happy, contented to be with friends and relatives, somewhere he wanted to be but could not. Such ideas often rest within the mind of the mass murderer (Holmes & Holmes, 1992).

CLASSIFICATION OF MASS MURDERERS

As with many forms of human conduct, sociologists and other social and behavioral scientists have attempted to organize the behaviors of mass murderers into social constructs. Such constructs are often based upon behavioral dynamics, motivations, victim characteristics and the methodology used in victim selection, locus of motivations (or the force behind the motivations), and anticipated rewards (Holmes & DeBurger, 1988, pp. 46-60). In the following subsections, we discuss these elements as they apply to mass murderers.

Behavioral Background: Basic Sources

There appear to be three root causes for the development of the mass murderer. As Levin and Fox (1985) point out, multicidal offenders' behavior cannot be explained by biological factors alone. Biological anomalies—whether brain disorders, problems caused by concussions, or chemical imbalances—do not explain a person's total personality and behavior (Norris, 1988; Podolsky, 1964). The same can be said of socioeconomic factors. The factors that were often described as root causes of delinquency in the late 1960s—poverty, female-headed families, and so on—do not explain or account for all delinquency, and no list of any such factors can explain mass murder. The following statement about serial murderers is applicable to mass murderers as well:

> "Bad" neighborhoods, economic stress, family instability, and violence in the culture do not directly produce serial murderers. Out of a cohort that experiences the worst possible combinations of social stresses, relatively few will engage in outright criminal behavior and fewer still will become homicidal. (Holmes & DeBurger, 1988, p. 48)

The elements that combine to create a mass murderer are as complex as those that result in a serial or spree murderer. Personality and behavior come about from a unique combination of genetics, socialization, and personal experience.

Donald Lunde (1977), a well-respected psychiatrist, boldly states that the majority of mass murderers suffer from psychosis and should be considered insane. He suggests that two kinds of personalities account for the overwhelming majority of mass murderers: (a) the paranoid schizophrenic, who displays an aggressive and suspicious demeanor and experiences hallucinations and/or delusions; and (b) the sexual sadist, whose murders are characterized by killing, torturing, and/or mutilating the victims in order to achieve sexual gratification. Lunde's second category does not fit the definition of mass murderer with which we are concerned here; rather, it describes what we refer to as a hedonistic serial killer (Holmes & DeBurger, 1988; Holmes & Holmes, 1998). It is likely that Lunde's categories were not intended to describe only the type of mass murderer under discussion here; he appears to have been concerned with multicide in general.

One further difference between mass murderers and serial murderers should be noted. According to our own analysis of more than 40 cases of mass murder, unless the mass murderer is a mercenary or has committed murder for revenge, he or she is usually willing to die at the scene of the crime, either committing suicide or forcing those in authority to kill him or her. (In cases involving disciple killers, their fates lie in the wishes of their leaders.) In contrast, there is overwhelming evidence that serial murderers do not wish to be apprehended; they wish to continue their killing.

Victim Characteristics

Victim traits do not appear to be a crucial element in mass murder. Victims are simply in the wrong place at the wrong time. The customers at that McDonald's restaurant had no role in Huberty's targeting them for mass murder other than simply being there.

Motivation

Another element used in the categorization of an individual mass murderer is motivation. What motivates someone to commit mass murder? This is not an easy question to address adequately. A partial answer rests in the locus of motivation, that is, whether it is intrinsic or extrinsic. For example, is the killer motivated by something deep within, something over which he or she has no control? This is a common statement heard in our interviews with serial killers. These killers identify an entity within their personalities that impels them to kill. It may, indeed, be a small part, but this 1% can take over the other 99% (Michaud & Aynesworth, 1983). This type of motivation does not appear to occur with mass murderers.

Sometimes, the motivating force rests outside the individual in the form of something that commands the killing. Charles Manson's control over Tex Watson and the other members of "the Family," as evidenced by the murders of Sharon Tate, Steven Parent, Abigail Folger, Voytek Frykowski, Jay Sebring, and Leno and Rosemary LaBianca, among others, is an example of an external locus of motivation. If Manson had not instructed the Family members to kill, they may not have done so on their own.

With James Huberty, the motivation to kill rested within Huberty himself. For myriad reasons, Huberty killed, but not because someone commanded him to do so. Rather, he apparently believed that society was operating against him; he perceived himself as a victim of social injustice. However, we will never know exactly why he chose to vent his rage on the strangers who happened to be at McDonald's that day.

Anticipated Gain

The murderer's anticipated gains must also be considered. What will the person gain by murdering? Does he or she want to get revenge on a former supervisor because of a poor job performance rating? Or, is a monetary reward anticipated, as when an arson-for-profit scheme results in the deaths of innocent people? Although murderers' anticipated gains can vary a great deal, the results are the same: Innocent people die.

Anticipated gains may be thought of as either expressive (psychological) or instrumental (material). Examination of the killer's perceived gains is important in the consideration of the type of mass killer, not only from a law enforcement point of view but also from a social/behavioral perspective.

Spatial Mobility

Geographic, or spatial, mobility plays a strong role in the categorization of four types of serial killers: visionary, mission, hedonistic, and power/control (Holmes & DeBurger, 1988, see Chapter 6). However, like victim selection, this element does not play a critical role in mass murder. Unless involved in mass murder for pay (e.g., arsonists or mercenaries), most mass murderers are geographically stable. The various cases of mass killers described above clearly illustrate this point.

An apparent exception to this usual trait of geographic stability is the case of the disciple killer. This type of killer, who has fallen under the spell of a charismatic leader, is often a runaway or a castoff from society. Such a murderer may not be indigenous to the area where he or she kills. However, the domicile of the disciple killer is often semipermanent, and victims tend to be people who live in the same locale as the killers and the leader.

TYPOLOGY OF MASS MURDERERS

The development of a typology of mass murderers is an arduous task. The first decision concerns the base number of killings necessary to call a case mass murder; as noted earlier, we have already settled on the number 3. The further requirement that the killings occurred at one time and in one place is easily met; there are many such cases.

The next task at hand is the development of a taxonomy predicated upon basic sources, victim characteristics, motivation, anticipated gain, and spatial mobility (see Table 4.3). There are also other elements to consider, such as type of weapon used, the lifestyle of the killer, relational closeness or affinity of the victims, and personal mental/physical health of the killer.

The Disciple

The disciple killer follows the dictates of a charismatic leader. The Manson Family provides many excellent examples of this type of mass killer. Consider Leslie Van Houten: A former high school cheerleader and beauty queen, this 16-year-old woman fell under the spell of Charles Manson, as did many others, including Lynette Fromme, Tex Watson, and Bobby Beausoleil (Livesey, 1980) (see Table 4.4).

What caused these apparently normal young people of the peace generation to become ruthless and merciless killers? There is no easy answer. We do know that disciple killers' victim selection is left to the discretion of

(text continues on page 74)

TABLE 4.3 Traits of Different Types of Mass Murderers

	Disciple	Family Annihilator	Pseudo-commando	Disgruntled Employee	Set-and-Run
Motivation					
Intrinsic		X	X	X	
Extrinsic	X				X
Anticipated gain					
Expressive	X	X	X	X	
Instrumental					X
Victim selection					
Random	X		X		X
Nonrandom		X		X	
Victim relationship					
Affiliative		X	X	X	
Strangers	X				X
Spatial mobility					
Stable		X	X	X	
Transient	X				X
Victim traits					
Specific					
Nonspecific	X	X	X	X	X

TABLE 4.4 Manson Family Members and Acquaintances

Charles Manson	Jesus Christ, Satan, the Devil, the leader of the Family
Susan Atkins	Involved in the Tate and LaBianca killings as well as other cases; also known as Sadie Mae Glutz, Sexy Sadie, Sharon King, and Donna Kay Powell
Bobby Beausoleil	Involved in the Gary Hinman killing; also known as Cupid, Jasper, Cherub, Robert Lee Hardy, and Jason Lee Daniels
Mary Brunner	First girl to join the family; may have been involved in the Hinman killing; also known as Marioche, Och, Mother Mary, Mary Manson, and Linda Dee Moser
James Craig	Pleaded guilty to being an accessory after the fact in two murders; formerly a state prison accessory
Lynette Fromme	One of Manson's earliest followers; assumed leadership after Manson was arrested; also known as Squeaky, Elizabeth Elaine Williamson; currently in prison for attempting to assassinate U.S. President Gerald Ford
Catherine Gillies	Granddaughter of the owner of the Myers ranch, where the family lived; wanted to accompany Watson and others the night the LaBiancas were killed; also known as Capistrano, Cappy, Catherine Myers, Patti Sue, and Patricia Anne Burke
Sandra Good	A Family member; also known as Sandy

Steven Grogan	Was with the murderers the night of the LaBianca killings; also involved in the Hinman killing and possibly involved in the attempted murder of a prosecution witness in the trial against Manson; also known as Clem Tufts
Gary Hinman	Befriended the Family and was murdered by them
Linda Kasabian	Accompanied the killers on the nights of the Tate and LaBianca murders; was a witness for the prosecution
Patricia Krenwinkel	Involved in the Tate and LaBianca killings; also known as Kate, Marnie Reeves, and Big Patty
Leslie Van Houten	Involved in the Tate and LaBianca killings; also known as Lu Lu, Leslie Marie Sankston, Louella Alexandria, and Leslie Owens
Charles Watson	Involved in the Tate and LaBianca killings; also known as Tex or Texas Charlie

SOURCE: Some of the information here is from Bugliosi (1975).

the leader. Manson allegedly told his followers to kill those who lived at 10050 Cielo Drive. This was the former residence of Doris Day's son, Terry Melcher, and actress Candice Bergen (Bugliosi, 1975, p. 4).

The anticipated gain of the disciple killer is psychological or expressive: The leader of the group demands the action, and the killer wants the acceptance of the leader. This psychological acceptance is paramount in the need hierarchy of the disciple killer. Money, revenge, and sex are neither motivating factors nor anticipated gains. The disciple killer desires psychological approbation and feels he or she deserves it for carrying out the wishes of the leader. This same scenario was repeated by the followers of Jim Jones in the massacre at Jonestown in Guyana. The hoped-for gain of the disciple killer is generally expressive (psychological) rather than instrumental (material).

Spatial mobility is also an element in the disciple killer's profile. Typically, the killer's acts of violence are carried out near the location of the leader. So, a disciple killer is rarely a traveler in the same sense as a geographically transient serial killer. However, as noted earlier, the disciple killer follows the leader and is unlikely to be originally from the general area in which the crimes are committed.

The types of weapons used in mass murder by disciple killers usually are restricted to hand weapons, such as knives and guns. In the Jonestown case, the weapon was poison.

Disciple killers, unlike other mass murderers, do not appear to have a general dislike of the world around them, nor do they believe that killing is the only way out of a particular situation. Disciple killers murder because of the effect that their leaders have on them. Their victims, typically strangers, are selected by their leaders, so victim selection is not a factor for disciple killers. In a way, these killers may be compared with soldiers who kill prisoners of war, not out of fear for their own lives, but because of their dedication to the message of the leader. Such killers may feel that they are relieved of a certain amount of personal responsibility by this scenario.

The Family Annihilator

Dietz (1986) describes the family annihilator type of mass murderer in an article titled "Mass, Serial and Sensational Homicides." This murderer kills an entire family at one time, and may even kill the family pet. According to Dietz, the family annihilator is the senior male in the family, often has a history of alcohol abuse, and exhibits great periods of depression.

The locus of motivation for this murderer is internal. Often feeling alone, anomic, and helpless, this killer launches a campaign of violence typically against those who share his home. Because of the despair in his own life, the killer wishes to change the situation and reacts in an extreme fashion.

Geographic mobility plays a very small role in this type of mass murder. The family annihilator tends to live in the area in which he commits his crimes. Usually a lifelong member of the community, he chooses to end the life of his family for reasons that are unclear not only to investigators but also to the killer. In Minnesota in 1988, David Brown allegedly axed four family members to death; there was no clear reason for his actions. In 1982, George Banks was arrested for shooting 13 family members and relatives for unknown reasons; the family was well known in the community. Ronald Simmons, recently executed in Arkansas for his crimes, killed 16 members of his family in 1986.

The Pseudocommando

Dietz (1986) also describes the pseudocommando, a mass murderer pre-occupied with weaponry. This kind of killer, usually male, often stockpiles exotic weapons in his home. Assault weapons, machine guns, even hand grenades are typical choices. The pseudocommando's mass homicide usually occurs after a long period of deliberation and careful planning.

There is no clear understanding of the exact etiology of the pseudo-commando personality. Certainly, there are social components to this behavior; the killer's world plays an integral part in his behavior. But the pseudo-commando lashes out at society in a most grotesque way. Something in his world is not correct and he decides to teach the world a lesson.

For the pseudocommando, as for most mass murderers, victim characteristics do not appear to be important in the victim selection process. Unlike the serial killer, who may have a shoe fetish or who may select victims with particular hairstyles, the victims of the pseudocommando may simply be in the wrong place at the wrong time. When Huberty walked into McDonald's in 1984, the only relationship he had with the victims was that they were all in the same place at the same time.

The locus of motivation of the pseudocommando appears to be internal. Something inside him compels him to carry out his massacre; there is nothing outside his personality that demands that he kill.

The anticipated gain of the pseudocommando is twofold. First, the activity of the mass kill calls attention to whatever issue the killer believes is important. In the case of Huberty, the economic condition of the nation that resulted in his moving to California from Ohio was certainly one of the reasons why he committed the act. The second hoped-for gain is less under-standable: The killer wants his name to live in infamy. Many of us recognize the name of James Huberty; how many of us know any of the names of the 40 victims? We can recall the name of Charles Whitman, but can you name any of his victims?

Geographic mobility does not appear to be a significant element among pseudocommandos. Huberty had moved to California, and Whitman lived in Texas. Both killed near where they were living at the time. The pseudo-commando does not seem to go far from home to commit mass murder.

The Disgruntled Employee

Disgruntled employees who kill have often been dismissed from their jobs or placed on some form of medical leave or disability. These mass killers are frequently receiving psychiatric counseling, and many see themselves to be suffering great personal injustices that are beyond their control. They retaliate for the wrongs they perceive by going to their former places of employment, searching out those they believe have wronged them, and kill-ing those people (and often others as well). This scenario fits the case of Joseph Wesbecker exactly, and also that of Patrick Sherrill. In 1986, Sherrill returned to the post office where he was an employee. Looking for super-visors, he started firing into the rooms and corridors of the post office, wounding and killing indiscriminately. Even though his primary motive was to kill supervisors, he actually wounded and killed many coworkers ("Crazy Pat's Revenge," 1986; "10 Minutes of Madness," 1986).

The psychological sources of the disgruntled employee's mentality are unknown. Typically, these people are on some form of medication and/or are receiving counseling or psychotherapy, and they are often diagnosed as paranoid.

The victim selection process of the disgruntled employee who kills is ini-tially nonrandom. This mass murderer seeks a particular group of people to kill, usually supervisors in the killer's former workplace. However, once inside the workplace, the killer often will fire randomly, shooting anyone who happens to be there.

Disgruntled employees' motivation to kill rests within their desire to "right a wrong." They kill to call attention to wrongs that they believe have been directed at and carried out against them. There is no external locus of motivation, as there is for the disciple killer.

The anticipated gains for this type of killer are psychological. There is no money to be realized, no social justice issues to be exposed, nothing outside the world of work and the injustices that were committed there.

The spatial mobility of this killer is usually very limited. Often, the per-son has been employed for years with the same company and has lived in the same community for that same period or longer. Joseph Wesbecker, for example, worked for the Standard Gravure Company for more than 15 years and was a native of Louisville. Patrick Sherrill was a postal worker for more than a decade and had lived in the same community for more than 20 years.

The danger that the disgruntled employee poses for citizens in the community at large is obviously quite limited; of course, this is of no comfort to the families of this killer's victims.

The Set-and-Run Killer

Another type of mass murderer described by Dietz (1986) is the set-and-run killer. Sometimes operating out of a motive for revenge, sometimes seeking anonymous infamy, and sometimes killing simply for profit, this type of murderer is qualitatively different from those discussed earlier.

As noted previously, most mass killers either commit suicide at the scenes of their crimes or force those in law enforcement to kill them. This is not true with set-and-run killers. These murderers employ techniques that will allow them to escape before the deaths they cause actually occur. For example, a set-and-run killer may plant a bomb in a building, setting a timing device so that he can be far removed from the scene when the explosion occurs. The person who poisons food products or medicines, placing the containers back on store shelves to be sold later, is also a set-and-run killer. This murderer does not directly observe the consequences of his or her acts; he or she may be across town or even in another country when the results become a part of the community's awareness.

Depending on the individual set-and-run killer's motivation, victim selection will vary. For example, if a person sets a building on fire so that he or the building owner who hired him can collect insurance money, and there are people inside the building who die as a result, the characteristics of these victims were of no significance in the crime; the anticipated gain of the arsonist is monetary. There is no psychological motivation in such a case, no attempt to show the world anything. This kind of motivation lies not within the personality of the killer but in instrumental gain.

In some instances, the victim of the set-and-run killer may be once removed. For example, consider a person who tampers with a food product made by Company X. Five people may purchase and eat the food, and all five may die, but in the mind of the killer, Company X is the victim because the company is believed to be at fault for the deaths. The motivation here is psychological; the killer is getting revenge on Company X for some perceived wrong. The anticipated gain is also psychological; no money is realized. A further psychological payoff for the killer is the fact that Company X may even lose money because some customers will no longer purchase its products, fearing that they are unsafe.

Because set-and-run killers are not present when their killings actually occur, they are very difficult to apprehend. Knowledge about the motivations, anticipated gains, and victim characteristics (when the victims are once removed) of these killers is crucial to those who hope to understand and possibly apprehend them.

CONCLUSION

The incidence of mass murder, both in the United States and abroad, does not appear to be decreasing. Certainly, there will always be people who will be motivated by personal, economic, or social pressures and who will arm themselves with a variety of weapons to carry out their acts. This is not an easy situation to accept, in no small part because of the perceived vulnerability it creates. We cannot protect ourselves from deranged mass murderers, or even, for that matter, from very rational, mercenary, set-and-run killers. This is unsettling, to understate the point. The mass murderer may strike at any time and in any place.

What can we do? Some say that effective gun control legislation may be an answer. Certainly, if rigorously and scrupulously enforced, such laws may deter some mass killers, who would resort to their own previously purchased weaponry to carry out their crimes. It would also deter those who recognize their feelings, plan their crimes, and then purchase weapons. Unfortunately, however, this scenario is not very common. It is unlikely that gun control can be society's answer to the problem of mass murder.

As discussed earlier, aside from paid killers, the majority of mass murderers display danger signs before they undertake their crimes. If we can become more aware of these signs, if those in the mental health profession, for example, know the red flags that may signal danger, then some of these acts can be circumvented before innocent lives are lost. This appears to be the best plan for the reduction of the horrendous crime of mass murder. Can it ever be completely eradicated? We can only hope.

CHILDREN WHO KILL

CHAPTER 5

There are few types of murders more difficult to comprehend than those committed by children. Fortunately, relatively few children kill. Yet there appears to be an increasing number of children who resort to fatal violence to resolve problems, either real or imagined. Nowhere is this more evident than in the recent outbreak of school shootings (Holmes & Holmes, 1999).

There are multiple examples of children who kill. Ted Bundy allegedly killed his first victim when he was not quite 16 (Holmes & DeBurger, 1988). Anne Marie Burr was an 8-year-old girl who lived close to the Bundys' uncle in Tacoma, Washington. Bundy supposedly took her to a small apple orchard, strangled her, and bludgeoned her to death. He is thought to have dumped her body in a ditch near her home that had recently been created because the public works department was constructing new sewers in the neighborhood (T. Bundy, personal communication, November 17, 1987). A relative of the young girl stated that she remembered that the original suspect was a 16-year-old young man. While the police were questioning the parents, Bundy was seen kicking dirt into the hole in their front yard where the sewers were being lain. Burr's body has never been found.

Peter Kurten, another serial killer, killed two children before he was 9 years old. He was playing on a raft with two friends, and he pushed one child into the water. The child could not swim and drowned. The other boy dove into the water trying to save his friend, but Kurten pushed him under the raft, and he died as well. Because no one witnessed the crime, no one suspected Kurten of being involved (Holmes, 1983).

Obviously, not all children who kill later evolve into serial killers. There are some who kill only once; others kill their parents or caretakers, and these are their only murders. Others continue with their killings. For example, Edmund Kemper, a serial killer, began by killing his grandparents when he was 15. Later, when he was 21, he was released from a correctional institution and killed at least eight other people, including his mother. He has been incarcerated since the late 1970s for this series of murders.

In Boulder, Colorado, a murder case made the headlines. The newspaper account described a courtroom scene of an 11-year-old boy standing patiently in front of the judge, with his hands in his pockets and his hair neatly parted to one side. The headline stated that the youth had killed his father with a .22 hunting rifle while the man slept. The child was angry because his father made him go to school. Murders such as this one are appalling, and they appear to be increasing. Such cases remind us all too graphically that children can murder, and they are doing it with more regularity than ever before.

In Hollywood, Florida, a young man went into the home of his elderly neighbors. Joseph Cotto said that he had an irresistible urge to kill his neighbors, Joseph Holzknecht, 78, and his wife, Mary Rose, 77. The police reported that there was no animosity between the killer and his victims. The killing was apparently well-planned: The young man entered their house on April 27, 1999, and stabbed them to death. He allegedly stole four credit cards, several $2 bills, and the couple's 1998 Ford. At the time of this writing, Cotto has not gone to trial.

There are other youthful killers, such as Michael Carneal, Eric Harris, Dylan Klebold, and Luke Wortham, who have started an epidemic of school shootings that have resulted in the deaths of their schoolmates. We have chosen to place these forms of mass murder in this chapter rather than the previous chapter because the focus here is on children who kill.

HOMICIDAL TRENDS AMONG YOUTHFUL KILLERS

It appears that the rate of homicide by children under age 14 has remained both stable and low when compared to other, older groups, such as children age 14-17. The homicide rate for 14- to 17-year-olds increased almost 150% from 1985 to 1993 (see Table 5.1). The Bureau of Justice Statistics, in its report *Homicide Trends in the United States* (Fox & Zawitz, 1999), says that since 1993 the offending rates for teens and young adults have declined somewhat, but still remain considerably higher than the levels of the mid-1980s.

It would be a grave error to categorize all juveniles alike. For example, the offending rate for children under age 14 changed little. But, as can be seen from Table 5.1, it is apparent that the rates for murder by the 14- to 17-year-olds exploded after 1984—surpassing the rates for 25- to 45-year-olds—going from a low of 8.5 in 1984 to a high of 30.2 in 1993. O'Brien, Stockard, and Isaacson (1999) report that in the past decade, youths aged 14-17 have been two to three times more likely to commit homicides than in the preceding 20 years. They stated that there are no definitive reasons for this increase, but they do suggest that children being born to unwed mothers appears to be a significant factor.

Table 5.2 contains data on race and sex for that same age cohort, which gives us a better picture of the data using these two traits as elements for examination. It is apparent that the males in the sample are more violent, which should come as no surprise to anyone. Furthermore, black males commit more murders and nonnegligent homicides than do white males. The same trend appears to apply to black females versus white females.

Concerning the years in this table, both white and black males were found to have committed their crimes at the highest rate in 1994. These rates were considerably higher than in 1976, when the rate for the white males was 10.4 and 72.4 for black males.

TABLE 5.1 Estimated Number of Offenders per 100,000 People Committing Murder and Nonnegligent Manslaughter, by Age Group

Year	13 Years and Younger	14 to 17 Years
1976	0.2	10.6
1977	0.2	10.0
1978	0.3	10.1
1979	0.2	11.7
1980	0.2	12.9
1981	0.2	11.2
1982	0.2	10.4
1983	0.2	9.4
1984	0.2	8.5
1985	0.2	9.8
1986	0.2	11.7
1987	0.2	12.3
1988	0.2	15.5
1989	0.3	18.1
1990	0.2	23.7
1991	0.3	26.6
1992	0.3	26.3
1993	0.3	30.2
1994	0.3	29.3
1995	0.3	23.6
1996	0.2	19.8

SOURCE: Material adapted from Maguire and Pastore (1999), p. 296.

Black females are uniformly more violent when committing these crimes than are white females. The murder and nonnegligent manslaughter rate for white females hovered between 1.0 to 1.7 per 100,000 people (the highest rate occurring in 1996). Black females reached a peak in 1991 with a rate of 12.1 per 100,000 population.

TABLE 5.2 Estimated Number of 14- to 17-Year-Olds per 100,000 People Committing Murder and Nonnegligent Manslaughter, by Sex and Race

	Male		Female	
Year	White	Black	White	Black
1976	10.4	72.4	1.3	10.3
1977	10.6	66.6	1.3	6.2
1978	10.7	64.5	1.2	7.9
1979	13.3	70.0	1.2	8.3
1980	13.6	85.2	1.1	8.0
1981	10.9	73.1	1.3	8.6
1982	11.3	61.3	1.2	5.9
1983	10.3	50.5	1.6	7.0
1984	9.4	47.6	1.2	6.2
1985	9.7	62.7	1.0	6.6
1986	12.3	72.2	1.1	5.6
1987	11.4	81.7	1.4	7.3
1988	13.9	111.9	1.0	7.4
1989	14.9	141.0	1.0	7.7
1990	20.6	175.3	1.5	7.5
1991	21.9	199.1	1.3	12.1
1992	21.8	195.2	1.4	11.1
1993	21.8	244.1	1.5	9.3
1994	22.4	266.7	1.4	9.7
1995	20.8	165.7	1.4	8.1
1996	17.4	134.8	1.7	7.8

SOURCE: Maguire and Pastore (1999), Table 3.136.

Obviously, there are racial and gender differences in considering murder and violence. Using homicide and nonnegligent manslaughter as the index of violence, males are more violent than females. But what, if anything, do these data say about victims?

TABLE 5.3   Homicide Victimization Rate From 1976-1997, by Age

Year	Age of Victim					
	Under 14	14-17	18-24	25-34	35-49	50+
1976	1.8	4.6	14.0	15.6	12.8	6.9
1977	1.9	4.9	14.5	15.7	12.5	6.7
1978	1.9	5.2	14.8	16.3	12.4	6.4
1979	1.8	5.3	16.9	17.8	13.0	6.8
1980	1.9	6.0	17.8	18.8	13.4	6.9
1981	1.9	5.1	16.3	17.8	13.2	6.9
1982	2.0	4.8	15.2	16.0	12.0	6.3
1983	1.8	4.5	14.0	14.8	10.7	5.5
1984	1.8	4.3	13.5	14.1	10.3	5.2
1985	1.8	5.0	13.5	14.2	10.1	5.1
1986	2.0	5.3	15.6	15.5	10.3	5.1
1987	1.8	5.8	15.7	14.9	9.5	5.0
1988	2.1	6.6	16.6	15.5	9.3	4.7
1989	2.1	8.0	18.4	15.7	9.3	4.6
1990	2.0	8.0	21.5	17.0	10.0	4.5
1991	2.1	11.3	24.4	17.0	10.1	4.6
1992	2.0	11.4	23.7	16.4	9.6	4.3
1993	2.2	12.3	24.7	16.3	9.6	4.3
1994	2.1	11.4	24.0	15.7	9.0	3.9
1995	1.9	11.2	21.9	14.1	8.3	3.9
1996	1.9	9.2	19.8	12.5	7.8	3.5
1997	1.7	7.5	19.7	11.6	6.9	3.2

SOURCE: FBI (1999).

The data in Table 5.3 suggest that the victims of homicide are usually older. For example, the age cohort of 18-24 poses a higher risk for fatal victimization than any of the other categories. From 1976 to the mid-1990s, there was an increase in the risk coefficient that was particularly visible in the age cohorts of 14-17, 18-24, and 25-34. The murder risk drops off over that same time span for the 35-49 and 50+ cohorts. But despite the changes in the rates, the pattern does not change with the age categories themselves.

THE ETIOLOGY OF THE
JUVENILE HOMICIDAL OFFENDER

There are substantial differences between causes and characteristics. For example, some claim that the main traits of serial killers include being a white male, in his early to mid-20s, and so on. But the reader must be aware that these are traits or characteristics rather than causes. Concerning juvenile homicide, we may be in a research position to add that murder will be more likely to occur on certain days of the week or with a particular type of weapon. The choice of weapon may also depend on whether the juvenile killer is affiliated with a group or gang, or if the juvenile acted alone. Klein (1995) studied gang versus nongang homicides and noted reasonable differences between the two, as shown in Table 5.4. In this chapter, however, we are dealing only with nongang homicides. There are excellent publications available for those interested in gangs and their perpetration of violence, including fatal violence (see Cummings & Monti, 1993; Hamm, 1993; Huff, 1996; Mays, 1997; Moore, 1978; Wooden, 1995).

Since the mid-1950s, there have been various efforts to explain the basic etiology of the youthful offender who kills. For example, some researchers have taken a biological or medical approach, examining juveniles who have experienced serious physical problems, such as epilepsy, EEG abnormalities, and limbic disorders, but they have all been relatively unsuccessful in fully explaining homicidal behavior. Other studies have examined the aspect of psychological control over homicidal behavior, but the controls investigated also appear to be grossly inadequate for circumventing the behaviors that result in murder.

In examining serious, violent juvenile offenses, the research most often cited comes from Wolfgang, Thornberry, and Figlio (1987), even though they were not able to explain the etiology of the juvenile offender entirely. There were serious shortcomings in this type of cohort research, but Wolfgang et al.'s strength lies in the fact that they did trace youth over a period of time and focused specifically on youthful offenders who were involved in serious crime. The shift in focus commenced with these studies and illustrates that children who are typically violent come from unstable, violent, or argumentative families and are influenced by the media (Inciardi, Horowitz, & Pottieger, 1997). Psychopathology may also play an important role in the formation of the youthful offender who kills.

Experts in the field have often relied on a diagnosis of mental illness to account for the perpetration of homicide by adolescents. McKnight, Mohr, and Quinsey (1966) studied juvenile killers who were all in a psychiatric setting at the time of the study. McKnight et al. found that the majority of the juveniles had psychiatric diagnoses that included epilepsy, manic depression,

TABLE 5.4 Gang Versus Nongang Homicidal Behavior

Behavioral Traits	Gang (n = 135)	Nongang (n = 148)
Gang homicides more often in the street	49%	34%
Gang homicides more often involve autos	64%	49%
Gang homicides more often involve guns	83%	68%
Gang homicides less often involve knives	24%	37%
Gang homicides more often include unidentified assailants	23%	10%
Gang homicides more often involve fear of retaliation	33%	9%
Gang homicides more often involve injuries to other people	23%	14%
Participants		
Gang homicides involve a higher average number of participants	6.96	3.77
Gang homicides more often involve victims with no prior contact with their assailant	49%	27%
Gang homicides are more likely to involve clearly gang victims	40%	2%
Gang homicide suspects are typically younger	19.40 years	23.68 years
Victims are typically younger	23.67 years	31.06 years
Gang homicide suspects are more likely to be male	94%	84%
Victims are more likely to be male	95%	89%
Gang homicide victims are more often Hispanic	53%	39%

SOURCE: Klein (1995).

schizophrenia, and psychopathic personalities (p. 185). Some 55% of the offenders were declared unfit to stand trial, and 27% were found not guilty by reason of insanity.

Other researchers have found similar results. Lowenstein (1989) found that psychological influences were found in children who kill, including low IQ, low levels of tolerance for frustration, a history of mental illness, low self-esteem, and severe problems in interpersonal skills and relationships. In contrast, Wolfgang and Ferracuti (1968) found that only 3% of the juvenile killers in their study were insane, not too far removed from the numbers found in a similar study by Wong and Singer (1973).

There are other studies that examine the role of the family in the basic etiology of the violent personality (Deykin, Levy, & Wells, 1987; Duncan & Duncan, 1971; Holmes, Tewksbury, & Holmes, 1999). These reports often cite an abusive background in the early years of the killer that may account for the later development of the victimizer as well as fatal predator.

In a recent study, Busch, Zagar, Hughes, Arbit, and Bussell (1990) compared a group of juveniles who killed with another group of nonviolent delinquents. The murder group contained 71 adjudicated youth (4 females and 67 males) between the ages of 10 and 17 (average age = 15.03 years). These authors found four background factors that differentiated the juveniles in the murder group from the nonviolent delinquent group: (a) criminally violent family members, (b) gang participation, (c) alcohol abuse, and (d) severe educational difficulties. Others who killed came from backgrounds that included family members who were violent inside the family itself, as well as members who were in jail or prison for violent offenses. These family members typically included fathers, mothers, aunts, uncles, and grandparents "who committed homicide, assault, battery, rape, armed robbery, stabbing, and shooting" (Busch et al., 1990, p. 484). In the same vein, Corder, Ball, and Hazlip (1976) report that abusive parents, chronic alcoholism on the part of the parents, incarcerations for criminal activities, and repeated hospitalizations for psychosis are elements found in the backgrounds of youthful homicidal offenders. They also mention that some affiliation with gang activities serves as a facilitator for homicidal behavior.

Another expert in the field of children who kill is Kathleen Heide. She reports in her book, *Young Killers: The Challenge of Juvenile Homicide,* using clinical case studies, that certain factors contribute to the increase in juvenile homicide since the mid-1980s. These factors are as follows:

- Child maltreatment

- Changes in family structure

- Absence of appropriate role models

- Violence saturation of American society

- Easier access to weapons

- A crisis in leadership and lack of heroes

- Increasing use of drugs and alcohol

- Rising number of young people raised in poverty

Youth who kill their parents are relatively rare, and Hillbrand, Alexandre, and Young (1997) report that this accounts for about 2% of all homicides. These researchers report that the typical killer of a parent or parents is

♦ a white male

♦ without a history of prior criminal convictions

♦ one who kills because of fear for his life

♦ more likely to kill the father with a gun

♦ one who often suffers from one or more major mental disorders

Despite the excellent research being done in this area of juvenile homicide, the younger adolescent (14 to 17 years old) appears to be the main problem for society and the criminal justice system. Additional research needs to be done on the etiology of this personality who resorts to fatal violence to resolve real or perceived problems.

There is another emerging problem involving juveniles who return to their school and shoot their classmates and teachers, and we explore this problem in the next section.

YOUTH KILLERS AND SCHOOL SHOOTINGS

Littleton, Colorado. Paducah, Kentucky. Pearl, Mississippi. Springfield, Oregon. Jonesboro, Arkansas. These are but a few cities and towns that have suffered a school shooting that resulted in the deaths of students and teachers. Such names as Eric Harris, Dylan Klebold, Michael Carneal, Luke Woodham, Kip Kinkel, Andrew Golden, and Mitchell Johnson have now become synonymous with this type of homicide. Each of these youths entered his school and murdered fellow students and, in two cases, his teachers. What can be said about the Michael Carneals, the Luke Woodhams, the Eric Harrises, and others like them? This is the focus of this section.

School Shooters: A Working Profile

In examining the cases of school shootings since 1996, a clear picture develops. Commonalities emerge, and they are strangely consistent (see Table 5.5). Thus, it is from these common traits that a profile can be drawn.

White Males

Seldom are females involved directly in school shootings. If a female is involved at all, it is peripherally, as a friend of the killer, as a member of a common clique, or as the procurer of a weapon.

Age

The age of the school shooter will depend upon the type of school— high school or middle/junior high school. In the cases listed in Table 5.5, the younger killers, Johnson, Golden, and Loukaitas, attacked their victims in middle or junior high schools. The other school shooters killed in their high schools. Therefore, the ages of the victims tend to be similar to the ages of the killers.

Student

The school shooter is typically a student at the school where the murders occur, although a shooter may return to a school that he used to attend. If this happens, then the school shooter is older, as in the case of a shooter in Stockton, California, who went into an elementary school in his neighborhood and killed several children.

Unlike adult mass killers, school shooters are not looking to murder strangers. There is some kind of relationship between a school shooter and his victims. The shooter and the victims are usually students and, in two cases, teachers at the same school. They are often acquainted, if not on a personal basis, at least in the sense that they have crossed paths in the hallways, classrooms, or cafeteria.

Rural or Suburban School Settings

Most school shootings occur in suburban or rural communities. In Kentucky, for example, the school shooting at Heath High School was in a small, western part of the state. In Jonesboro, Arkansas, the middle school is located near the borders of Missouri and Tennessee, many miles from the state capital, Little Rock. Littleton, Colorado, is a suburban town of Denver,

TABLE 5.5 Selected School Shooters

	Michael Carneal	Mitchell Johnson	Andrew Golden	Kipland Kinkel	Luke Woodham	Barry Loukaitas	Eric Harris	Dylan Klebold
Age	14	13	11	15	17	14	18	17
Sex	Male	Male	Male	Male	Male	Male	Male	Male
Race	White	White	White	White	White	White	White	White
Weapons	5 rifles 1 handgun	13 handguns	13 handguns	Rifle	Baseball bat Rifle	Rifle 2 handguns	30+ bombs Rifle Pistol 2 shotguns	30+ bombs Rifle Pistol 2 shotguns
Number of assaulted victims	8	15	15	29	10	4	48	48
Type of school attacked	High school	Middle school	Middle school	High school	High school	Junior high school	High school	High school
Number of murdered victims	3	5	5	4	3	3	13	13
State	Kentucky	Arkansas	Arkansas	Oregon	Mississippi	Washington	Colorado	Colorado

and Springfield, Oregon, is a small community close to Eugene, which is itself not exactly a metropolis.

When a shooting does occur in an urban school, it is usually aimed at a personal enemy of the killer. Certainly, you can find any number of shootings that occurred in an inner-city school where a troubled student settled a personal score with violence. But for our purposes here, the latter example is an example of a shooting in a school, not a school shooting. Drugs, personal vendettas, and so on play more of a role in these kinds of shootings. Therefore, the character and the motivation for the killings in an urban school environment are different from the motivations and the anticipated gains in the school shootings in this chapter.

Middle-Class Background

The school shooter typically lives with his family in a middle-class environment. Carneal's father is an attorney. Dylan Klebold lived with his parents in a million-dollar housing development. Eric Harris lived close by in a subdivision where the homes were more modestly priced, but still in the six figures. Klebold drove a BMW, and Harris drove a Honda.

These are not youths who come from deprived backgrounds. There is no daily concern for survival. Their economic futures appeared bright and secure, with college an educational goal for the family. Kip Kinkel's sister was in college at the time of the shooting. Klebold's older brother attends the University of Colorado in Boulder. Their families had bought into the American dream. The school shooters, however, abandoned that dream and chose to end their formal education, and sometimes their lives.

Disenfranchised Youth

The personal histories of school shooters are amazingly similar. For example, the students who turned violent are often disenfranchised from the student body. Other students at the school typically tell reporters and police that the shooters were "weird" and outcasts of the student body. At school, they were often teased and tormented. Luke Woodham, for example, stated that he was often victimized by the popular students in his high school for reasons unknown to him. Thus, many of these students are considered strange or different by the other students. The killers reinforce these differences by behaviors that are judged antisocial. For example, when bowling, the Trench Coat Mafia of Littleton, Colorado, would salute each other and greet each other with "Seig Heil" when a member bowled a strike. This kind of behavior serves two purposes. First, it alienates the other students and onlookers, and second, it serves as a solidarity mechanism for the members of that out-group.

Out-Group Membership

This kind of youthful violent offender will often become involved with other disenfranchised young people. They may start their own group as a rebellion against the groups that already exist within the school. Luke Woodham cited his affiliation with others who were Satanists. Harris and Klebold belonged to the Trench Coat Mafia, a group that had its own uniform—long black coats, black boots, and chains.

The out-group has its own identity and interests, and it fulfills a psychological need for the youths. Unable to find or keep friends within the school community, the members seek others who share their values, prejudices, and antisocial propensities.

Interest in the Internet and Computer Games

The shooters often explain to law enforcement how they spent long hours on the Internet or played certain computer games. Many of these video games are violent, with plenty of shooting, maiming, and killing. The two killers in Littleton were reported to have played such games in both boys' homes. Friends said they were very competitive, even with each other.

The shooters often join chat rooms on the Internet and converse with others with similar interests. They are often familiar with various Web sites that cater to their psychological needs. At the time of the Littleton killings, there were at least 32 Web sites devoted to hate messages. The police confiscated the killers' computers and retrieved valuable information from the hard drives.

Interest in Weaponry

School shooters are often fascinated by exotic weapons and bombs. In the latest school shooting in Colorado, the young men placed bombs in the school cafeteria. Weapons were found in the home of one of the young men, among them a sawed-off shotgun. In Jonesboro, Arkansas, the father of Andrew Golden took his son on hunting trips as a young child. And as a 5-year-old, Golden posed as a cowboy with a rifle taller than himself.

As the saying goes, guns do not kill people, people kill people. These killers usually have access to guns. One young killer stole a gun from his grandparent, and in the Littleton case, a female friend of one of the killers is suspected of purchasing a gun for him. The killers use their wits and friends to acquire weaponry to accomplish their designated missions.

Regardless of where they acquire their weapons and the knowledge of how to use them, these youthful offenders have an interest in weaponry, if for no other reason than to carry out their mission to kill. Some have also learned how to construct bombs from instructions available over the Internet, as was suspected in the Oklahoma City bombing case of Timothy McVeigh and Terry Nichols.

Foretelling of Fatal Events

Like other mass killers, school shooters will often tell others of their plans to kill. Eric Harris and Dylan Klebold in Colorado told fellow students that "something" was going to happen on Hitler's birthday. Michael Carneal brought two guns to school the day before his fatal shootings. Kip Kinkel told a student that he planned to plant a bomb under the bleachers and block the doorway so students could not get out. He added that he would also go into the cafeteria and shoot people with his .22 gun because he had more rounds for that weapon than he had for his 9 mm pistol. This student paid little attention to the comments, thinking that Kinkel was just trying to sound important.

It is apparent that young shooters often forewarn of their actions, but they may not be taken seriously by the students who are privy to those comments. If the shooters typically make strange comments or pronouncements, other students may believe that these warnings of violence are just more of the same.

Secrecy

The daily activities of the shooters prior to the fateful day are often shrouded in secrecy. If acting alone, the killer has retreated to a private personal space. Typically, he spends huge amounts of time playing video games and planning his attack. If the killer murders with an accomplice, they share their time with each other. Klebold and Harris spent days together making bombs that they apparently hoped would not only destroy the school building in Littleton, but would also kill a multitude of victims.

Amazingly, the killers are usually able to keep their activities and interests from others. The parents are surprised when they discover that their child was making weapons and bombs in the home. Secrecy aids the planning and the implementation of the attack.

Motivation

There are mixed motivations in the mind of the school shooters. Some of them hate particular minorities, school groups, or racial groups. Others may want revenge for perceived personal wrongs. In the latter case, for example, Michael Carneal went to his school to kill those who had insulted or demeaned him, including his girlfriend, with whom he had recently broken up. This breakup could have been a precipitating factor in his decision to return to school and kill his fellow students.

The motivation, then, rests within the killer's personality. There may be others within the killer's group who are aware of the impending disaster, but the decision to kill is made by the offender. The motivation serves not only as an impetus for action, but also as a rationale. In the mind of the killer, there are no true innocents. All of those he murders deserve to die. By killing a few, millions will hear of his actions and recognize his name. Thus, there is a certain amount of economy involved in this form of mass killing. Would any of us know the name of this child if not for the school shooting?

Abandonment of Former Friends

Because of his experiences at school, such as personal rejections, teasing, and so on, the school shooter will eventually abandon his former friends. Typically, he finds acceptance, solace, and comfort with members of an out-group, who accept him for himself because they share many of the same attitudes and values. Some shooters attach themselves to groups that are devoted to a hate message, whereas others, like Luke Woodham, affiliate themselves with groups involved in the occult or other groups that are on the fringe of society's acceptance.

TREATMENT OF VIOLENT JUVENILE OFFENDERS

Little progress has been made not only in the understanding of the violent juvenile offender but also in the treatment of such youths. One impediment to treatment is that the child is often almost an adult when he or she comes before the criminal justice system. This is true not only in the United States but in other countries as well. For example, Rydelius (1988) reports that in Sweden the average age of the youths who appeared before the court was 16 (but there is no mention of when the acts themselves occurred).

One strategy that might aid in the reduction of juvenile homicide is early intervention. It is important that we identify not only the personal and social traits of the children who kill but also strategies to deal with the problem effectively once these children have been identified.

One treatment strategy that has been used with some success is the therapeutic wilderness camp program. In such programs, usually for youths aged 12 to 17, the adolescents attend therapeutic sessions, both individual and group counseling; take part in group "trust adventures"; and participate in other activities designed to build self-esteem, trust, and so on. Boot camps are also popular. However, boot camps are usually reserved for the less violent juvenile (G. Vito, personal communication, November 28, 1999).

The success rate of the various treatment programs will vary with different factors. Of course, one of the factors that would almost guarantee success is control of the intake. If the program decides to permit only a certain group of offenders to enter—say, first-time nonviolent, intelligent offenders—then that program would probably have a higher success rate than programs that must take whomever the court commits.

CONCLUSION

Presently, there is tremendous concern regarding the growing violent crime rate among our country's youth. Juveniles today appear to be increasingly violent. Despite official statistics that tell us that crimes by juveniles have fallen 33% since 1993, murder and nonnegligent homicide rates for children have remained rather constant (Mashberg, 2000). Nevertheless, we are incessantly reminded of how violent youths can be by national media reports of high-profile cases such as school shootings.

At the time of this writing, two youths were accused of plotting the bombing of their school in Port Huron, Michigan. In this case, they were charged as adults for conspiracy to commit murder. Prosecutors state that these youths were planning to top the death toll at Columbine to make their crime even more infamous ("Boys Accused," 2000). And in California, two Summerville High School boys were arrested for planning a similar assault on the Columbine anniversary date ("Police Arrest Students," 2000).

It has been reported that school violence is down, and official statistics of murder and school-associated deaths also appear to show a decline. According to the Justice Policy Institute in Washington, school-associated violent deaths fell from 43 in 1997-1998 to 26 in 1998-1999. And during the school year 1999-2000, only 19 school-associated deaths have been tallied (Mashberg, 2000). Despite these empirical findings, the public's perception of the problem is quite the opposite. Today, parents are more concerned than ever with the safety of their children in school and in other places where children assemble openly.

Despite the reason for optimism with regard to youths who kill, more research needs to be conducted on this phenomenon. Studies need to examine not only those who execute their plan, but also those who conspire to kill. It is only when we have a firm grasp on the exigencies that motivate a person to take others' lives, and possibly their own, will we be able to treat these individuals and rehabilitate them to become effective, functioning members of the larger society.

INTIMATES WHO KILL

There is a thin line between love and hate. One of the most joyous moments in a person's life is when that person finds someone with whom to share time and life. Weddings are a testament to that. This commitment is also witnessed when people decide to share a home and announce their relationship to their friends, families, and acquaintances. Too often, though, this relationship results in abuse, violence, and even death.

In Pittsburgh, Pennsylvania, for example, Timothy Boczkowski was convicted in 1996 for the 1990 death of his first wife, Elaine. He was already serving a life sentence but was subsequently convicted in 1999 for the 1994 murder of his second wife, Maryann (J. Whitt, personal communication, June 14, 1999). In Atlanta, William Reese killed his wife in April 1999. He had a long history of abuse directed toward his wife, Rosemary. In one case, Reese tied his wife to their bed with an electrical extension cord. She worked herself free hours later and ran to the police. Like many wives, she pleaded that the charges against him be dropped after his arrest. But some may say that justice was served in this case: Reese died in an explosion when he pulled out a natural gas line while attempting to stage the crime scene as an accident. In a bizarre case, Scott Falater admitted stabbing his wife 44 times but claimed that he was sleepwalking at the time. He also admitted holding her head under water in their backyard swimming pool as she was dying from her wounds. The jury did not accept his story, and he was found guilty in her death. Attorney Thomas Capano was convicted of murdering his mistress and dumping her body at sea. His defense was that another of his mistresses accidentally killed Anne Marie Fahey and he helped only in the disposal of the body, which he placed in an ice chest and dumped at sea. Capano received the death penalty in Delaware.

Of course, not all acts of violence against an intimate companion are fatal. In March 1999, Pricilla McMurrian, age 31, slashed her ex-husband's penis with a knife. She stated that he was bragging about the sexual escapades he had had since their separation, including the night before the attack. McMurrian was charged with second-degree battery, and at the time of this writing, no legal disposition has been made.

Why an intimate relationship between two people turns violent is not fully understood, despite the efforts made by researchers dedicated to finding reasons for this violence (see Gelles, 1974; Gelles & Straus, 1989; Hansen & Harway, 1993). Some are convinced that wife abuse in particular is a further manifestation of society's general devaluation of and violence against women (Stordeur & Stille, 1989). In any case, although they differ as to the estimates, most researchers agree that victims underreport spouse abuse.

This chapter examines partner homicide, the killing of one partner by the other. Although most people think of the family as a safe and emotionally warm setting for all members, this is not always the case. We present some statistics on the prevalence of spouse abuse and partner homicide below, and then we examine the criminal justice response to this form of homicide.

STATISTICS ON PARTNER HOMICIDE

The abuse of partners is not confined to the United States. For example, Came and Bergman (1990) state that in Canada 30 women per year are killed by their partners. In England, Smith (1989) reports that a woman is killed every 3 days at the hands of her husband or boyfriend (p. 1). But these numbers pale in comparison with the victimization of domestic partners, especially women, in the United States.

The government reports that each year 1 million women suffer nonfatal violence by an intimate (Bureau of Justice Statistics, 1995b, p. 3). This is a conservative estimate when one compares that suggested number to the American Psychological Association's (1996) figure of more than 4 million women (p. 10). To further compound the situation, the American Psychological Association estimates that one in three adult women will suffer some form of physical abuse sometime during their adulthood (p. 10). Of course, most of the victims of domestic abuse are women; the Bureau of Justice Statistics report that only about 5% of all victims are men (Bureau of Justice Statistics, 1994b).

Additionally, there is a growing body of evidence that shows that partner abuse is also quite prevalent in the gay and lesbian communities. For example, it is estimated that about 25% to 33% of homosexual couples are involved in some form of abuse (Barnes, 1998, p. 25). Translating this into numbers may mean that as many as 100,000 lesbian women and 500,000 gay men are battered by their intimates. To add insult to injury, Murphy (1995) says that there are more than 1,500 shelters and safe houses for battered women, many of whom routinely deny their services to victims of same-sex battering.

In terms of numbers for heterosexual intimates, in 1993, approximately 575,000 men were arrested for committing violence against women, and about 49,000 women were arrested for committing violence against men (American Psychological Association, 1996, p. 10).

Dealing specifically with homicide, it may be that the homicide is the culmination of an escalating history of physical, sexual, and emotional abuse. Note some of the following findings:

- If a woman is murdered, it is twice as likely that she has been killed by an intimate partner (Bureau of Justice Statistics, 1996).
- A Florida study determined that almost 9 out of 10 murder victims had a history of domestic abuse (Florida Governor's Task Force, 1997, pp. 46-48, tables 14-21).

- In almost half of the cases, the murderer had threatened previously to kill the victim or to commit suicide, and in almost one third of the cases, police had been called to the home to intervene (Florida Governor's Task Force, 1997, pp. 46-48, tables 14-21).

- Whereas almost 5% of the victims of domestic abuse are males, 70% of the victims of intimate homicide are females (Bureau of Justice Statistics, 1994a).

- In almost 6 out of 10 cases, husbands who were killed by their wives precipitated their own deaths by being the first to use physical force or to threaten the spouse with a weapon that was often the batterer's own property (Browne, 1987, p. 10).

- The Bureau of Justice Statistics reports that of female homicide victims killed in 1992, their relationship to the killer was known in 69% of the cases. Of this 69%, 28% were killed by their spouse, ex-spouse, boyfriend, or ex-boyfriend. Of male homicide victims killed in 1992, their relationship to the killer was known in 59% of the cases. Of this 59%, 3% were killed by a spouse, ex-spouse, girlfriend, or ex-girlfriend (Bureau of Justice Statistics, 1995a).

One sad element in many partner homicides is that often the police have been called several times previously to the homes in which fatalities later occur (Buzawa & Buzawa, 1990). Our own communication with veteran police officers from several states indicates that in 80% to 95% of partner homicides, the police had been called to the home at least once during the 2 years preceding the incident. In more than half of these cases, they have been called five times or more. This is a significantly higher rate than that reported in the Florida study. In interviewing women in Kentucky's maximum security prison, 50% of the inmates who were incarcerated for murder or manslaughter had killed their partners (who had repeatedly assaulted them). These women had sought police protection numerous times before resorting to murder. One prison official estimated that of the women she had counseled at the prison, she believed that almost 50% of them had been battered by their significant others (authors' files). In the majority of cases, the murders resulted from the women's attempts to protect themselves or their children (D. Stephens, personal communication, July 28, 1999).

It appears that only a small percentage of battered women kill their spouses to end the violence. Some are eventually able to leave their abusive relationships, and some continue to suffer, unable to break the cycle of violence or to leave. There is no way to gauge accurately the number of women, or men, who are involved in abusive partnerships and never resort to fatal

One young woman, Linda H., 21 years old, was arrested and sentenced to 25 years in a Kentucky prison for the murder of her common-law husband. She related her story to the authors:

> "I was first married when I was 17. It wasn't a good marriage, and Tom and I got divorced in a year. But I already had Bobby [her son] when we broke up.
>
> "Me and John met up a month after I left Tom. John was no good. He was a drug dealer and a coke head. I knew that when I moved in with him, but I did it anyhow.
>
> "Things were a little rough, really, from the beginning. He hit me a few times, and I would just take it. He was good to Bobby, so I thought it would all turn out all right.
>
> "One night, he got high and started to hit on me. He then hit Bobby and threw him across the room against the wall. Something just snapped in me. It was one thing for him to hit me. I wasn't going to let him beat up on Bobby. So I went into the bedroom and got his gun and shot him, and I shot him again.
>
> "No, I'm not sorry. I miss my son. He's staying with my parents until I get out. I just couldn't let him beat up on Bobby. Could I?"

violence. There are many who keep the abuse secret and never make it public. What is known, however, is that the number appears to be rising (Gelles & Straus, 1985).

Who Is at Risk?

In domestic relationships, the roles and interactions between the two partners are complex. Nevertheless, it is important to understand the nature of the relationship in order to evaluate it. Roles such as husband and wife, friend and lover, are complex. Behavioral expectations and anticipated gains can be unclear and difficult to sort out. However, when partners' expectations of their relationship are not fulfilled, violence can result. The manifestation of that violence is bordered by the moral and legal responses that exist in a society. In other words, societal responses to those who resort to fatal domestic violence can set the tone for the continued exercise of violence by others, or for its diminishment. We must examine the motivations, potential gains, and potential losses incurred by those who commit partner homicide in order to understand this phenomenon.

For years, too many assumptions have been made regarding the relationships, motivations, and anticipated gains that result in partner violence. For example, many have assumed that both partners are at equal risk for domestic homicide. However, research indicates that there are definite gender differences in risk level. Women are at greater risk of being killed by their spouses than are men (Kratcoski, 1987). The physical strength of the male is only one possible explanation for women's risk. Another is that men are more likely than women to have high stress scores on psychometric tests, and the source of the stress is more likely to have resulted from traumatic losses in the men's lives (health or job) or other, very painful psychological experiences. These losses or experiences occur typically before the homicidal incident (Kratcoski, 1987). On the other hand, homicides committed by women against their spouses are more likely to be linked to domestic stress and are often preceded by a history of wife abuse. In the cases of both husbands and wives, it appears that those who resort to fatal violence within the family are unable to respond adequately to high levels of stress (Kratcoski, 1987).

In dealing with the stress of repeated abuse at the hands of their partners, many women exhibit uniform behavioral and psychological responses to their perceived (and, in most cases, real) danger. The outcome of these perceptions is an accumulation of a great deal of anger, which is not always directed toward the abuser. In many cases, abused women direct their anger inward, and it manifests in suicidal behavior, poor self-image, drug abuse, and alcoholism; on rare occasions, it takes the form of stigmatophilia (self-mutilation) (Fishbain, Rao, & Aldrich, 1985; Lester, 1987).

Location of Crimes

In partner homicide, there are interesting differences between the sexes as to where the murders occur. One reason may be the availability of the weapon used. Also, routine activity may play an important role in the site of the murder as well as the weapon used (Messner & Tardiff, 1985). For example, in almost 90% of the cases of partner homicide, the murder occurs within the home (Browne, 1986; Kratcoski, 1987). The location of the murder within the home appears to be related to where the individuals spend the most time or where they most often come into confrontation. For example, Mann (1988) found that women who commit partner homicide are most likely to kill in the living room; the next most likely place is the bedroom, followed by the kitchen. Men who kill their partners, however, do not show any such pattern.

Weapons Used

The methods and weapons used in partner homicide vary widely: knives, guns, poisons, rifles, blunt instruments, asphyxiation, and explosives have all been used, as have the murderer's bare hands. Handguns are often readily available, and this has caused some to question how much this availability might contribute to the incidence of partner homicide (Browne, 1987). Some proponents of gun control, for example, stress the importance of stronger legislation regarding the purchase of handguns as one method of reducing partner murders, but there are conflicting opinions on this issue. Howard (1986) has examined the gun control issue from the perspective of family law. Considering that a firearm is used in most cases of partner homicide, she reports two interesting hypotheses:

1. Spousal homicides are spontaneous crimes of passion that result from momentary rages arising from the heat of circumstances rather than from a fixed determination to kill (p. 64).

2. If deprived of guns, partner killers either would not substitute another weapon or would substitute a weapon less lethal than a gun (p. 66).

From this perspective, gun control legislation would have a direct impact on the rate of partner homicides, at least for those committed by males. However, research findings concerning the impact that such legislation would have on the rate of partner killings by *women* are unclear. Research has shown that women who kill their partners often use knives (in part, perhaps, because of the place-specific nature of the weapon used, and the fact that many such homicides take place in the kitchen).

For women in precarious living situations, the gun may be the "great equalizer." For example, a woman using a knife as a murder weapon exposes herself to a greater risk of successful resistance by her male partner because she must approach within arm's length of him to use it. Using a knife instead of a gun may render her defense ineffective and result in her becoming the victim, perhaps with fatal consequences. Browne (1986) notes that 81% of women who kill their abusive mates use guns; knives are the weapons in such cases only 7% of the time.

Men who kill their partners do not show a preference for any one kind of weapon. For men, the murder weapon may be incidental to their motivation and the location of the attack.

PERPETRATOR PROFILES

Women Who Kill

Although some women do kill their partners for other reasons, most who kill are responding to some form of attack. These women often have histories of long-term abuse at the hands of the men they kill (Florida Governor's Task Force, 1997; Mann, 1988).

Goetting (1987), who studied 56 women arrested for spousal abuse in Detroit between 1982 and 1983, lists the following characteristics in a profile of the female killer:

- Black
- Early or mid-30s
- A mother
- Lived with the family
- Uneducated
- Unemployed
- Prior arrest record

This list of traits differs significantly from the list of traits of women who have been abused by their partners without the abuse resulting in death. The Commission on Domestic Violence (American Bar Association, 2000) reports the following:

- Race is not indicative of batterings. It crosses all racial lines.
- Women ages 19 to 29 are most battered; women over 46 are the least battered group.
- Past and current victims of domestic abuse are overrepresented in the welfare recipient category.
- Many of the women are unemployed because of interference by the partner at the victim's place of employment.

Keep in mind that this list of traits represents female victims who have not been murdered. There may be other elements that would be partly responsible for abusers who decide to murder.

Goetting's (1987, 1989) research also suggests that the women who kill often commit their crimes after a series of arguments or volatile confrontations with their slightly older partners. The final argument typically takes

April

placc in the bedroom or living room between 2:00 p.m. and the early morning hours. The image that emerges from the research is one of a woman who is disadvantaged along several dimensions, including a sense of personal and social isolation. These women often live in loosely structured relationships with men and are poorly equipped to succeed in their daily struggles for survival. They are mired in a world in which they have few social, educational, and personal strengths to help them rise beyond their limited social world. The women are viewed as victims in a male-dominated world and in a society that is structured to be conducive to success for men (Goetting, 1987, 1989).

An earlier study (Barnard, Vera, Vera, & Newman, 1982) offered more traits of battered women who kill, but only the last traits seem to differ from Goetting's work. These women

- Suffered frequent and severe verbal abuse
- Were victimized by often brutal assaults
- Were threatened frequently with death
- Had a history of suicide attempts
- Were better educated than their partners
- Lived apart from their partners

Browne (1987) stated that most of the women in her sample of more than 300 women came from families in which they were themselves abused as children, typically by their fathers. These same findings are reported by Korbin (1986) and Conway (1989). Ironically, these women later married husbands who were similar in personality traits to their fathers. These researchers also note several predictors that might lead women to resort to fatal violence in a domestic setting:

- The severity of the woman's injuries
- The man's drug use and frequency of intoxication
- The frequency of abuse
- Forced or threatened sexual acts by the man
- Suicidal threats by the man
- Threats to kill made by the man

Women may blame themselves when placed in a situation of partner homicide. According to statistics, only a small number of women involved in domestic abuse ever resort to homicide as a resolution to what they see as a hopeless position. Women who are the victims of long-term abuse tend to develop feelings of helplessness and anomie, which may be even more difficult for them to fight (Walker, 1979). Also, the marriages of battered women tend to adhere to strict gender roles, with dominant men and submissive women (e.g., see Hansen & Harway, 1993; Stordeur & Stille, 1989). It may be that these women strike back only when they see no other way to end their suffering.

Researchers such as Lenore Walker have described the cycle that spouse abuse, most often wife abuse, typically follows (Walker, 1979, 1989). Each incident of abuse may be divided into three stages. The first stage, the prebattering period, is a time of increasing strain between the victim and the batterer. The abuser may make verbal assaults, attack inanimate objects (especially the victim's possessions or other items she values), and engage in minor acts of violence against the victim. The victim may respond by trying to calm or placate the abuser. The goal is to defuse the potentially dangerous situation.

If the nonbattering partner is successful, the matter will stop here. However, if this fails, or if the anger is too great, the second stage, violence, will occur. Here, both parties have lost control of the situation. The batterer lashes out in a rage, often causing serious injury, and the victim can only endure the abuse at this time.

In the last stage, with the rage spent and the victim showing obvious injuries, the batterer tries to console the victim. He may beg for forgiveness, promise to try to resolve the problem (e.g., quit drinking or avoid certain people or situations), or promise to seek counseling. These conciliatory gestures rarely last, however, and the cycle soon starts again.

A woman is more likely to leave an abusive relationship once the rate of positive reinforcement (the promises made in the third stage of the cycle) decreases. This point of separation, once reached, is risky for both partners. It poses such a threat of abandonment that a man may kill his partner rather than let her leave. Conversely, a man who prevents his partner's leaving may jeopardize his own life. In these cases, the woman who turns on her mate is typically attempting to escape. She does not intend to kill, just to prevent him from blocking her escape or to keep him from hurting her again.

There may be a paralyzing terror in the relationship at this point. As noted earlier, battered women build up high levels of anger, but they "rarely experience their anger directly" (Howard, 1986, p. 77). Although they often direct their aggression inward and appear to be passive receivers of their abuse, "passivity and denial of anger do not imply that the battered woman is adjusted to or likes the situation. It is the last defense against homicidal rage" (Howard, 1986, p. 77).

Men Who Kill

Men who kill their partners are typically quiet and want to be accepted by society, but they are unable to relate to the world around them and exhibit a great deal of stress in their daily lives (Smith, 1989). Men involved in partner homicide often were reared in families that emphasized keeping a stiff upper lip in the face of personal adversity. These men also have a great deal of difficulty expressing their emotions (Smith, 1989).

According to Humphrey and Palmer (1987), homicide offenders are more apt to have experienced considerable losses throughout their lives, such as parents who died or were separated from them by divorce, abandonment, or institutionalization. Later in life, they experienced difficulties on the job, probably changed residences frequently, and often went through changes in marital status. These stressful events can combine to spark homicidal attacks, usually on people whom the offender fears losing the most, such as a spouse, a child, or a close friend.

Men who feel unable to control their lives outside the family are particularly likely to exert control within the family, especially over their female partners. As Sylvie Schrim, a Montreal attorney, stated, "I am continually dealing with men who want to control the women in their lives, who view their partners as some kind of property" (quoted in Came & Bergman, 1990, p. 18). If such a man is placed in a situation where his partner is striving for personal autonomy (which he perceives to be at his expense), whether inside or outside the relationship, he may see violence as his sole answer to the problem. Killing is an act of ultimate control over his partner.

Long-lasting periods of stress become an integral part of the psychological compulsion to lash out fatally. This point is illustrated by Humphrey and Palmer (1987), who report that men who become murderers often do so as a result of prolonged frustration. In their sample, they found that the lives of the killers were more stressful than the lives of the nonkillers, and the stress was endured over a longer period of time.

Weiner, Zahn, and Sagi (1990) note that there are significant differences between men who commit partner homicide and men who do not. For instance, men who kill their partners are more often drug abusers, are more prone to abuse alcohol, are more often intoxicated, and are more frequently given to verbalizing physical threats and exhibiting violent forms of physical behavior than are other men. Tragically, men who murder their partners are also more likely to have been emotionally, physically, and/or sexually abused themselves as children. They are also more likely to commit sexual violence against their partners than are males not involved in partner homicide.

THE LAW AND LEGAL DEFENSES IN CASES OF SPOUSAL HOMICIDE

The law does not regulate behavior in a social vacuum. There are performers in this arena of criminal justice who all play vital roles. Historically, wives were viewed as the property of their husbands, to do with as they so desired (U.S. Commission on Civil Rights, 1982). The laws have changed radically in this area, reflecting a changing sense of priorities and fairness. The U.S. Attorney General's Task Force on Family Violence (1984) recommends that the determination to take legal action should be guided more by the form of abuse and less by the relationship between the abuser and the victim. This statement has been construed to extend beyond the traditional family to nontraditional relationships as well.

Law Enforcement

The police officer on the beat is usually the first to respond to the domestic disturbance call. The common reaction for many officers in the past was to separate the quarreling couple, diminish the hostility, and simply allow the two people to cool off. For years, this approach was part of the prevailing wisdom on domestic violence. However, in many cases, when the police took this approach, returning to the house time after time, the situation had not improved, and the end result was partner homicide. Now, jurisdictions have adopted a different strategy. In Kentucky, for example, the police may make an arrest even if the offender's partner does not wish to press charges. If the officer believes that a danger exists to one partner, this provides the needed justification. Factually, every state allows its police to arrest those suspected of misdemeanor domestic violence incidents on probable cause, and more than half of the states and the District of Columbia have laws requiring police to arrest on probable cause for at least some domestic violence crimes (Zorza, 1995, p. 66).

It is estimated that as many as half of all cases of partner abuse that later result in partner homicide are never reported. What is known is that only about one case in seven is reported to the police (Florida Governor's Task Force, 1997, p. 3). The Bureau of Justice Statistics estimates that when the woman was physically injured she reported the incident slightly more than 50% of the time. When she was not injured, she was less likely to report the crime (Bureau of Justice Statistics, 1995b, p. 5). Clearly, a concentrated effort needs to be made to improve the reporting of domestic violence, and for this we need a greater understanding of the reasons behind the failure to report. Some victims, for example, may not report abuse because of fear of personal reprisals or the negative stigma attached to such a public admission. Others may not report abuse because of possible repercussions for their status in the community or their positions in the workplace. Despite the many possible reasons for victims' reluctance to report their abuse, those who are involved in abusive relationships clearly need to be encouraged to do so.

One further note on this issue: Historically, police officers have been reluctant to respond to domestic disturbance calls. Horror stories are continually told of the personal risks that these officers face. However, our own data analysis indicates that police officers actually are at greater personal risk in responding to robbery calls than to domestic disturbances.

Prosecutors

The National Woman Abuse Prevention Project concerns itself especially with the relatively low rate of spouse abuse cases that are reported and then later prosecuted. Perhaps this low rate is a reflection of the previously common position taken in society that what goes on within the domestic sphere, even abuse (which may later turn to partner homicide), is a private concern best left to the parties involved to resolve. Whatever the reasons, prosecutors frequently fail to send spouse abuse cases forward for judicial deliberation. Some prosecutors believe that domestic violence is a low-priority issue, and all that a couple needs is a cooling-off period. Violence between spouses is often not viewed in the same manner as violence between two strangers. Some prosecutors even discourage battered partners (male or female) from seeking judicial deliberation. They may belittle the merits of the cases, either deliberately or unintentionally, and thus convince the victims that they have little chance of a successful resolution.

If a case does go forward for deliberation, some prosecutors may plea bargain cases involving serious battering down to misdemeanor status. This sends a message to those who batter that this type of crime is not taken seriously by those in the legal system. Because the cases are not prosecuted as diligently as they should be, offenders are often released from custody and return home to commit more acts of abuse, and sometimes, partner homicide is the consequence.

It is also the case that some victims simply refuse to testify against their abuser because of fear of reprisals or a reluctance to share intimate secrets of their lives. From a prosecutor's position, there are no easy steps to follow in order to achieve a successful resolution in a battering case. There is no magic wand to wave to protect the abused and to prevent further bias.

However, certain key elements of a successful prosecution response have been identified. After these guidelines were implemented in San Francisco, the National Woman Abuse Prevention Project reported a 44% increase in the conviction rate of felony cases, a 136% increase in the number of cases in which charges were filed, and a 171% increase in the disposition of domestic violence cases there (Soler, 1987). Greater success in intervention by the criminal justice system in abuse cases should sharply reduce the number of partner homicides committed.

The Judicial Response

In domestic violence and partner homicide cases, as in all court cases, judges have the primary role of ensuring that the law is followed. However, judges are also involved in the highly subjective task of sentencing, and in cases of spouse abuse, the sentences they pass sometimes reflect their own ignorance of the severity and the potential for escalation of domestic violence.

There is a common assumption that all judges are wise, analytical, and learned, but this is not always the case. Too few judges who must preside over cases of domestic violence are cognizant of the intricacies of human behavior. Their educational training has been focused on the law, and, for the most part, any education they may have had in human behavior came in their undergraduate years, in introductory psychology and sociology courses. The psychology of the battered spouse and of the partner murderer is complex.

The task of defending in court a woman who has killed an abusive partner is formidable. In many cases, the men posed no immediate threat to the women at the time of the killings, yet the women insist that they killed in self-defense. Self-defense laws generally require a perception of imminent danger, and they do not take into consideration the reasonableness of the prediction of imminent danger based on a history of repeated acts of violence (Simpson, 1989; Walker, 1993). Psychologists disagree with this legal standard and argue that battered women may reasonably expect their partners' anger to escalate quickly because experience has taught them to recognize cues of pending abuse. Many argue that being the victim of years of abuse can lead to a person's showing symptoms not unlike those found in posttraumatic stress disorder. Lenore Walker calls it *battered woman syndrome* (Walker, 1983, 1984, 1989). In recent years, some states have allowed a legal defense in such cases called the "battered woman self-defense," which is based on the premise that a woman suffering from bat-

tered woman syndrome may perceive herself to be in danger when no imminent threat is apparent (Walker, 1983).

Currently, the self-defense statutes in most states also include an equal
force requirement, which assumes that the parties to a physical struggle are
of equal size and have equal experience with using parts of their bodies to
defend themselves. Hence, when a battered woman uses a weapon to defend
herself against a physically stronger man who uses fists, her legal account-
ability raises from a misdemeanor to a felony. However, because women are
generally smaller than men and are not socialized to defend themselves physically the way men are, weapons may be seen as necessary elements in
women's self-protection.

Public policy regarding domestic violence has changed greatly in the
past decade, and psychologists have played an active role in this transforma-
tion. Court testimony by expert witnesses has refuted many myths about
domestic violence, such as that battered women are masochistic and stay
with their mates because they like to be beaten, that violence fills a deep-
seated need that attracts partners to each other, and that because battered
women have free will they can leave a relationship if they choose to do so.
These myths have prevented battered women who kill their abusers from
receiving impartial trials.

Since the mid-1980s, expert testimony on battered woman syndrome
has been allowed in many states in cases of women accused of killing their
partners. Some states do not have self-defense laws, and, in these states, even
the belief that one is in dire or fatal danger is not considered an adequate
defense for the commission of homicide. Even in a state where self-defense
may be recognized, "perfect" self-defense requires the perpetration of fatal
violence to be necessary and reasonable. If a person's attempt at self-defense
is deemed to have involved unnecessary or excessive force, then he or she
cannot be freed on grounds of self-defense. If the amount of force used in
self-defense is found to be necessary and reasonable, even if it resulted in the
death of the attacker, then it is deemed to be "perfect" self-defense, and
there is no finding of guilt.

Sometimes, the outgrowth of a self-defense plea is a finding of
"imperfect" self-defense; this is often the case in manslaughter. The case of
State v. Thornton (1987) provides an example. In this case, a man came home
unexpectedly and found his wife in bed with another man, whom the husband then killed. He was charged with first-degree murder. The charge was
later reduced to voluntary manslaughter because the court found that
(a) there was adequate provocation, which caused (b) extreme anger and rage;
(c) there was no opportunity to cool off; and (d) there was a causal connection between the provocation, the anger, and the fatal act. Legal precedent

has established the circumstances under which men and women may react with fatal force, as well as how the courts perceive that behavior.

It is unclear what, if any, particular direction the courts are taking in deciding cases of domestic violence. Some legal decisions point toward a relatively classic approach; others indicate a turning toward a philosophy that may be called the "medical model," which takes into account such concepts as battered woman syndrome, posttraumatic stress disorder, and battered woman self-defense. In some parts of the country, for example, women are incarcerated for partner homicide; in others, they are granted probation or their cases are dismissed. In other words, there is a lack of consistency nationwide in the adjudication of partner homicide.

It should be noted that there are some researchers who claim that the character of partner homicide is changing. Wilbanks (1983), for instance, asserts that women who kill their partners are becoming more deliberate in their murders and that their extent of planning is more complex. If this is true, such a shift will have an influence on the law and on litigation in cases of partner homicide. In a controversial conclusion, Mann (1988) has gone so far as to state that women who kill may indeed be the victors in domestic fights and that the question of self-defense deserves reexamination.

POLICY IMPLICATIONS

Ideally, the criminal justice system operates smoothly and efficiently in dealing with the various personalities and politics that enter into court cases. Too often, however, the system does not succeed. In one case in the early 1980s, for example, a young mother in a southern state was strangled by her partner. This attack occurred after she had been subjected to a series of increasingly violent attacks by her partner. He was convicted of manslaughter rather than murder because the court decided that there was sufficient provocation to somehow mitigate the circumstances. He served less than 5 years in prison on this charge.

This was not the only time that this defendant had been before the court. Earlier, the court had issued an injunction against him, prohibiting him from having any contact with his partner; he promptly violated that injunction. He was arrested for that violation but was released. His violent assaults upon the woman continued, but the system did little to aid her. Law enforcement's response to the increasing violence was ineffective. The woman was given no protection, and she died at the hands of this man despite the court's order prohibiting personal contact and despite the arrests made by the police. The case simply fell through the cracks and resulted in her brutal murder.

As noted earlier, the police have been reluctant to become involved in domestic disputes. Historically, they have arrested abusers only if the victims have been willing to press charges. In many areas, the law has now been changed to allow investigating officers to make a determination of abuse and to act legally upon that determination. This is a positive step.

Sentencing in cases of spousal abuse typically has been light. Sometimes, prosecutors "undercharged" the perpetrators. In cases that do not result in death, the victims often decide not to pursue prosecution, and cases are dropped. In still other cases, plea bargaining results in reduced charges.

More shelters for abused women are needed. Many are overcrowded, and some women have no other place to go for their own safety and the safety of their children. For an abused woman to return home—the place where the abuse occurred—usually means that the abuse will continue.

Solutions to the very serious and complex social problem of domestic violence are beyond the scope of this chapter. Clearly, both abusers and their victims are in need of education, as are those in law enforcement and the judicial system who must deal with the potentially fatal results of such violence. The police, who are typically a citizen's first introduction to the criminal justice system, must be educated about the cycle of abuse and about such concepts as battered woman syndrome and victim blaming. The actors in the court system, from attorneys to judges, must also be made aware of the elements of psychology and complex human behavior involved in cases so that they do not make judgments based on myths and prejudices. Those in the corrections profession must also be informed of the problem of partner homicide and the special issues and behaviors presented in such cases.

CONCLUSION

Partner homicide and domestic violence are very complex, multifaceted problems. They are not well understood by the general public, and, unfortunately, myths and misinformation surround them. Currently, social and behavioral scientists are making important advances in the understanding of partner battering, domestic violence, and spousal homicide. All of the behavioral dynamics are still unclear, however, and there has been limited progress toward the ultimate goal—the solution of the social problem of partner homicide.

Mere treatment of the aftereffects of the violence is insufficient. Better techniques need to be formulated that will result in early identification of both potential offenders, who may one day resort to fatal violence, and potential victims, who may one day be homicidal statistics. Better educational programs, more effective counseling techniques, and better understanding of the total problem are needed if there is to be an effective reduction in partner homicide.

PARENTS WHO KILL

The family is usually thought of as a haven and a place of warmth and caring, but it also can be a setting for many different kinds of violence, abuse, and even murder. One type of crime that is coming more and more to the attention of law and policymakers is the murder of children. The extant literature examining the distribution of homicides of children has found that its occurrence is not distributed randomly throughout the population (L. Baron, 1993). Studies have found that the reported killings of children are more common in impoverished, urban areas with a greater concentration of ethnic minorities (Abel, 1986; L. Baron, 1993; Christoffel, Anzinger, & Amari, 1983; Copeland, 1985).

Suggestions attempting to pinpoint the nature and causal variables of the killing of children have centered on abuse. It is commonly believed that parents who are abusive toward their children are at a greater risk of killing their children. Research generally supports the notion that most children who die at the hands of their parents are victims of physical abuse. For instance, Spungen (1998) found a direct correlation between the child abuse rate and the number of child homicides. However, the literature does not appear to support the notion that parents who sexually abuse their children are at any greater risk of murdering their children than any other group (see also Mohr, Turner, & Jerry, 1964; Revitch & Weiss, 1962; Righton, 1981; Virkunnen, 1981).

For most of us, it is almost impossible to imagine any case where we could harm our own children, let alone kill them. The killing of defenseless children is a crime that almost everyone can agree is one of the most serious offenses that anyone can commit. However, homicide is one of the top five causes of death of children in the United States (Christoffel & Liu, 1983). Cross-nationally, official statistics tell us that the murder rate for babies appears to be higher than the murder rate for the general population (Lester, 1991). In fact, the United States ranks second among developed nations in the child homicide rate (Christoffel & Liu, 1983). The killing of children galvanizes public attention, and yet it occurs more frequently than anyone would like to admit.

One of the best ways to begin to understand the murder of children by parents is to conceptualize this problem as part of a larger issue, domestic violence. A recent report from the Bureau of Justice Statistics (Greenfeld & Snell, 1999) found that of the 60,000 murders committed by women between 1976 and 1997, slightly more than 60% were committed against intimates or family members, whereas in the 400,000 murders committed by men, only 20% were against family members or intimates. Furthermore, of all the murders committed in which children were the intended victims, half were committed by the victim's own parents (Marzuk, Tradiff, & Hirsch, 1992).

One of the first studies that looked at the killing of children by parents was conducted by Resnick (1969). In this study, he found that mothers were twice as likely to kill their children as fathers and that approximately 30% of all child homicide cases were committed against children under 6 months old. This finding is not surprising given that the killing of newborn children by parents (infanticide) is an age-old crime and was practiced regularly in ancient times and in this country as late as the 1700s (Empey, 1978).

CHAPTER 7

THE MURDER OF CHILDREN IN
THE UNITED STATES TODAY

One does not have to look far to see cases where a parent killed his or her child. Only recently, for example, a young father in Florida (Richard Adams) was arrested for killing his infant daughter. In the famous case of Susan Smith in South Carolina, Smith claimed that a black male carjacked her car and took her two children. After appearing on national TV and begging the carjacker to spare the lives of her two sons, she confessed to strapping her two children in their car seats and letting the car roll into a local lake. In another case in Arkansas, a young mother was arrested and charged with the murder of her infant daughter. An apparent believer in the occult, she had "burn sacrificed" her daughter so that the child's soul would become the property of the devil (C. Chastain, personal communication, 1992).

The stories noted above are, indeed, exceptional cases. And yet in the media today, we hear more and more stories about impoverished women or those who are down on their luck who escape the stressors associated with rearing their children by killing them. Presently, there is no evidence to suggest that women today are casting aside their traditional roles as nurturers and committing more violent crime, including murder. For instance, Greenfeld and Snell (1999) found that since 1990 the number of felony convictions in state courts for homicides committed by women has fallen 4% (see Table 7.1). They also report that of all the females arrested in 1998, 11% were arrested for homicide, with females committing two murders to every one where the victims were under the age of majority.

Public Condemnation of the Murder of Children

It is clear that the murder of children is not condoned by the majority of our society. The professional and academic literature is replete with examples of prison inmates who are victimized themselves because they violated

TABLE 7.1 Percentage of Homicides of Children Under Age 5, by Relationship With Offender

Year	Parent	Other Family	Friend/ Acquaintance	Stranger	Unknown
1976	57	8	19	3	12
1977	59	6	20	4	10
1978	57	6	22	4	11
1979	47	9	23	4	17
1980	54	7	21	3	15
1981	57	8	24	2	10
1982	58	4	22	2	13
1983	59	5	23	2	11
1984	52	8	26	3	11
1985	62	5	24	2	8
1986	56	6	24	1	13
1987	58	6	23	2	10
1988	53	6	27	1	13
1989	57	7	22	2	12
1990	52	6	24	1	16
1991	54	6	24	3	13
1992	53	4	25	4	14
1993	50	4	28	3	15
1994	52	5	25	3	14
1995	52	7	24	6	11
1996	50	6	30	2	12
1997	57	6	24	2	11
1998	56	4	27	1	12

SOURCE: FBI (1999).

118

children. Although this condemnation applies to members of both genders, society has an especially difficult time with women who intentionally kill their children. The cases of Pamela Smart and Carolyn Warmus illustrate how fascinated the American public is with women who commit murder. However, the coverage given these women in the national news media pales in comparison to that given the Susan Smith case.

In this chapter, we present some of the research findings concerning parents who kill their children. Some studies have proposed particular social and psychological profiles that may be useful for mental health practitioners and criminal justice professionals who are working toward both the early detection and apprehension of these offenders.

CHILDREN AS CHATTEL AND INFANTICIDE

Historically, children have been seen as chattel, that is, as the property of their parents, especially fathers. In some societies, children are viewed as such until they reach the age of maturity, at which time the child is then supposed to act like and be treated as an adult.

In some countries, families living under subsistence conditions actively participated in infanticide as one way to combat the economic problems associated with clothing, feeding, and educating their children. Thus, to protect their ability to care for the already existing family members, parents (often mothers) who could not afford to raise a new infant would kill the child soon after birth. Killing female children was especially prevalent because daughters often were not seen as an economic asset to the family. A daughter required a dowry at the time of her marriage, payable to the groom's family. The dowry was supposed to provide for the economic burden that the male would assume in taking care of the female. Thus, for families that did not have sufficient resources, the killing of infant female children served three purposes. First, it allowed the family to care more fully for existing family members. Second, it allowed the family to care specifically for male children, who would work someday to help provide sustenance for the family. And third, it removed the future need to provide a dowry (Whitehead & Laub, 1989, p. 41).

Other reasons suggested for infanticide center upon the stigma attached to bearing children out of wedlock. Historically, the lives of children, especially illegitimate children, were viewed cheaply. For instance, Rose (1986) found that because of the social and economic vulnerability of unwed mothers, illegitimate children were more likely to be killed by their mothers than were legitimate children. This trend can be traced through the 19th century.

In the United States today, the birth of illegitimate children does not carry with it the social stigma of years past. Mann (1984) states that women who kill their children today do so to relieve themselves of an unwanted burden. National and international statistics point to the fact that children under the age of 1 are at four times the risk of becoming a victim of homicide than are children of other age groups (Rose, 1986).

Other current research has supported the notion that those who kill their children often fall into economically depressed categories. For instance, Hawkins (1986) reported that the homicide rate for black youth is 3.7 times higher than that of white youth (Hawkins, 1986). As illustrated in Table 7.2, recent government statistics appear to support this finding. In fact, the current data show that for child victims killed by their mothers, black women kill their children about 3.9 times more often than do white women (Greenfeld & Snell, 1999). These figures do not mean that the black community holds its children in less regard than do other groups, but the figures may point to potential causes, such as economic inequality and poverty, as a principle reason for killing newborn infants.

Over the centuries, families have also resorted to many other means of dealing with children who present problems. At one time, abandonment had the same effect as killing a child. Children were sometimes sold into involuntary servitude or placed in apprenticeship programs away from home so that they would not be a financial burden on the family. In other words, families have a long history of attempting to relieve themselves of unwanted or troublesome children. Financial strain has most often been at the center of these problems. Today, the stresses that lead to the murder of children appear to have changed. For example, in recent interviews with women in the United States who have killed their children, the primary reason appears not to be financial hardship, as in other countries, but inconvenience. These women believe that, with the children, they are no longer attractive to men, and the children's care appears to get in the way of their social lives. Regardless, as we will show in the following sections, parents do still kill children whom they believe cause them hardship.

TYPOLOGY OF THE CHILD-KILLING INCIDENT

Before we begin to discuss the typical individual, situational, and environmental factors that may lead to the murder of children by their parents, a clear differentiation of terms is necessary. Resnick (1969) created a typology of child homicide to help us better understand and differentiate between the different types of child murder and the motivation of the offending parent. These two different categories are *neonaticide* and *filicide*.

TABLE 7.2   Homicide Rate of Children Under Age 5, by Race (in percentages)

Year	White	Black	Other
1976	2.4	10.2	3.2
1977	2.3	10.4	2.2
1978	2.5	10.6	2.5
1979	2.3	8.8	3.8
1980	2.4	9.4	2.2
1981	2.4	8.4	2.5
1982	2.5	9.5	3.2
1983	2.2	9.7	2.5
1984	2.3	8.1	2.0
1985	2.3	8.1	1.4
1986	2.5	11.5	2.4
1987	2.4	8.6	2.2
1988	2.4	10.2	1.3
1989	2.6	9.2	2.2
1990	2.5	9.3	2.0
1991	2.7	11.3	2.9
1992	2.4	9.8	1.6
1993	2.4	11.3	2.7
1994	2.6	10.2	2.0
1995	2.6	8.8	1.7
1996	2.7	9.5	2.3
1997	2.3	8.0	2.2
1998	2.4	8.1	1.2
Average	2.4391	9.5217	2.2696

SOURCE: FBI (1999).

Neonaticide

Neonaticide occurs when a child who is less than a month old is murdered. Parents who commit neonaticide are typically younger and have completely different motivations from those who murder older children (Resnick, 1970). The parent who murders an infant child does so deliberately and with forethought. To these offenders, the thought of the additional social and financial burden that will be placed on them is too much to handle. In the majority of these cases, the child is strangled or suffocated by the mother shortly after birth and is often placed in a plastic bag and disposed of in a trash receptacle.

Filicide

On the other hand, there is filicide, or the murder of older children. When parents commit filicide, there is often some evidence of physical abuse. In many cases, a parent loses control and strikes out at the child through either physical violence or shaking, which can cause permanent harm or even death. In cases of filicide, the parent often does not mean to harm the child, but the result is still death.

Types of Filicide

Understanding the difference between neonaticide and filicide is extremely important. Just as important is a clear denunciation of the types of filicide, each of which has different motivations. Pitt and Bale (1995) break down the types of filicide, and those perpetrated by parents as battering deaths, homicides committed by the mentally ill, retaliation homicides, mercy killings, and killings of unwanted children.

Battering deaths. In 1995, there were 1,215 documented cases in which children in the United States died from child abuse or neglect (Whitmire, 1996). This figure represents a 40% increase from 1985 (Frankel, 1996). Thus, it is no surprise why one of the most cited reasons for the death of a child is physical abuse (Ewing, 1997). When the death results from a case of child battering, the parent often has never understood any other way to discipline the child than corporal punishment. Furthermore, the offending parent was often a victim of violent child abuse as well. In these cases, the parent tries to discipline the child, loses control, and beats the child to death. Such was the case when Kayla McKean was killed for soiling her pants.

For those of us who are parents, it is easy to understand the stressors of parenthood. Babies, especially young and colicky ones, may cry for hours at time with little or no relief. Because the infant cannot communicate with its parent, the parent can only guess at what might be wrong. The repeated soiling of pants, or even a child's failure to keep a room clean, may cause the parent great distress and could lead to violence. Even if the parent was not physically abused as a child, he or she may lose control and shake the baby in an effort to quiet it, which can result in permanent brain damage and possibly death. It is estimated that 20% to 25% of infants who are victims of shaken baby syndrome die as a result (Topping, 1996).

Homicides committed by the mentally ill. A second type of filicide is committed by a mentally ill parent, although this is not a common occurrence. Typically, it happens when an impaired parent is left unattended with the newborn child. Sometimes, the impaired parent may give the child a bath or may assume that the child is capable of performing a number of functions that the child simply cannot do on its own. One of the reasons why this type of child homicide appears to be so rare lies in the definition of homicide. It is clear that the impaired parent did not mean or intend to kill the child but simply failed to provide the correct supervision or support for the infant. Rarely are these cases treated legally as homicides, even though they do involve the death of a young child at the hands of its parent(s).

Retaliation homicides. In retaliation homicides, one parent retaliates against the other parent, especially if that parent is planning to leave the family, by intentionally killing their child. In ancient times, if neither of the two parents could decide on custody, then the child was split, with each parent given custody of half of the child's corpse. Even the story of wise King Solomon relates such a tale. In this case, two women claimed to be the mother of a child. When they went before Solomon, he proposed to cut the child in two and give each mother half. Finally, one mother broke down upon understanding that the child would die in the process and pleaded with the king to let the other woman have the child. Solomon then awarded the child to the mother who was willing to give up the child because only a mother's love could run so deep.

Mercy killing. A third type of filicide is mercy killing (Pitt & Bale, 1995). As stated previously, mothers or parents of children with visible or noticeable physical or mental birth defects may kill their children to spare them the pain and humiliation of growing up in a harsh world. The interesting thing about mercy killing is that many of those considered part of this genre do not involve any visible physical or mental defects at all. Some parents may dispose of their children because of their belief that the world is just too harsh a place for anyone to live. They believe that if they were to raise their children, their chances of success in life would be so low that it would be better to send them to where they can live a happy and fruitful life with their God of choice.

Murder of unwanted children. The final category of filicide that we discuss here is the murder of unwanted children. At least in media circles, this type of killing appears to be growing at the highest rate. Every year, the public is besieged with cases where a young high school girl has no idea she is pregnant and finally gives birth either in the shower or at a high school prom. These young women often have no idea how they would raise a child, nor do they completely understand how the introduction of this child in their lives at this time will affect their future opportunities. In many cases, these children are born, suffocated, and tossed aside. Although we have no idea how many cases in the United States today fit this profile, when a case like this is brought to the attention of the media, the story usually runs for several days nationally, with a longer play in the region of perpetration.

MOTIVES FOR MURDERING CHILDREN

Just as it is important to understand the types and classifications of child killings, it is equally important to understand the motivations behind them. We have already noted several of the common reasons given for murdering children, but a full description may be in order.

The actual motivations behind child homicide can be understood only in light of the totality of the circumstances in which both the child and the offending parent live. As such, there will probably never be universal agreement on the motivation for murder. In any event, some have offered some possible explanations as to why a parent might kill his or her child.

Altruism

In some cases, parents may take the life of their child or infant for altruistic reasons. In cases like these, the parents, at least in their own minds, wish to prevent the child's suffering from either a real or perceived abnormality. Children who are born with birth defects or are clearly mentally impaired from birth used to be the prime candidates in the United States and in many Third World countries in the past. In the case of a mentally disabled child, a Siamese twin, or a child born with a harelip, the parents may view the killing as a mercy killing, wishing to spare the child the embarrassment and humiliation of growing up with such an obvious disability (Resnick, 1969). Although current research tends to show that these children can lead healthy and happy lives, the parents may feel that the likelihood of this happening to their child is slim to none.

Removal of the Impediments

The second motive often cited by those who kill their children is that their acts removed the impediment (the child) from blocking their career and professional aspirations. A parent may kill the child who is the product of an extramarital affair in order to keep it secret, or the woman has offers for marriage or a relationship with a man only if she parts with her children (Resnick, 1969).

Accident

The third most common motive cited for the parental killing of a child is simply that the death was an accident. These type of homicides are usually the result of what has been labeled "battered child syndrome" (Kempe, Silverman, Steele, Droegemueller, & Silver, 1962). Often, the child does something he or she has been warned against, and the parent punishes the child by using physical violence. This violence ranges from shaking a baby, to leaving the child alone in the bathtub, to suffocating the child or damaging the child's larynx by a firm grasp on the neck, to beating the child to death. In most cases, the offending parent is not alone, and the other parent or a friend may be present. The key to understanding this type of homicide is the realization that the parent did not intend to take the child's life.

The preceding discussion focused almost entirely on the types of motivations of parents who kill. Given these results, it seems fairly obvious that the most common reason given for killing a newborn baby is that it is unwanted, whereas the most common reason for killing an older child is some type of misguided altruism. Even with these intentions, it does us little good in describing these types of actions and their corresponding motivations without providing a typical profile of the men and women who kill their children. This is the focus of the next sections.

MOTHERS WHO KILL

Women who kill represent a challenging dilemma for agents of the criminal justice system. Society does not expect women to engage in serious criminality or possess violent and aggressive tendencies, but some women do. In fact, Bromberg (1961) stated that women in the modern world are "no strangers to the crime of homicide" (Bromberg, 1961, p. 39). Recent statistics published by the Bureau of Justice Statistics (Greenfeld & Snell,

1999) show that of all of the women arrested between 1976 and 1997, 11% were arrested for murder. Although this statistic does not provide us with the breakdown of the victim-offender relationships, it has been reported that between 1976 and 1997, parents and stepparents were responsible for the murder of nearly 11,000 children, with mothers and stepmothers committing about half of them. Greenfeld and Snell (1999) noted that in cases where the mother was the killer, 52% of the victims were sons or stepsons, as compared to 57% when the father was the killer. Furthermore, mothers were responsible for a higher number of children killed at a young age, whereas fathers were more likely to have been responsible for the murders of older children.

In a study examining homicides committed by women, D'Orban (1990) validated past assumptions concerning sex and murder. For example, murder was found to be almost exclusively a male action. Other studies have found that males commit almost three of every four murders. What is interesting about these statistics is not that females are less likely to commit homicide but, rather, who the perpetrator chooses for a victim. In general, females are more likely to kill intimates, whereas males are more likely to kill strangers. For instance, D'Orban found that in 80% of cases, the female murderer kills someone within her own family. And of that 80%, 50% of the victims were her own children.

Historically, the same patterns appear to hold. In the past, women were more likely to have killed their unwanted or deformed children rather than their husbands or other family members. Contemporary reasons believed to account for mothers killing their children include accidents, postpartum depression, and psychosis.

Adding to the qualitative difference in homicides committed by both men and women is the belief that females who commit murder are more likely to be suffering from some form of mental illness or other personality disorder (D'Orban, 1990). This finding, however, appears to be contingent upon the type of victim chosen. Those mothers who kill their children because they are an impediment to future goals often show no signs of depression, nor do they typically display personality defects before the incident. They are also unlikely to commit suicide after the incident. However, Resnick (1970) found that about one third of mothers who kill their older children also kill themselves.

Further research looking at the psychology of the female child killer found that 7 out of 10 parents who killed their children were mothers whose actions were triggered primarily by psychosocial stressors. These psychosocial stressors included abandonment by the husband or family and loss of financial support for their own or their children's survival (Bourget &

Bradford, 1987). Other research has found that less than 24% of the cases were a result of either an accident or mental incompetency[1] (Goetting, 1995).

There are definite risks to children, depending largely on the social stresses and unique social experiences to which the mother is exposed. Risk factors also include the child's age, birth order, and gender. The second author conducted an analysis of records in the state of Kentucky on mothers who murder their children, which yielded some interesting data. The results of this research are not unlike those of other studies that have been conducted on samples from other regions of the United States. We report the results of the Kentucky study in the following section.

Mother's Age and Risk to the Child

One of the important correlates of a mother's propensity toward fatal violence against her child is her age. Younger mothers are usually less mature than older mothers, and they often find it difficult to keep pace with their own lives, much less care for the needs of a child. These young mothers are less likely to have the coping skills and abilities needed to take care of an infant on their own, and they are also less likely to have a social support network (e.g., family, spouse, peers) to help. The pressures on a young mother can lead to depression and despair, and may be one of the precipitating factors why these women lose their tempers and kill their children. Other research, such as that conducted by Mann (1993), found that younger mothers tended to kill children under the age of 2, whereas older mothers killed children older than 2. This is consistent with the possible lack of maturity among young mothers and the possibility that mental illness or incompetence is more prevalent in older perpetrators.

Mother's Marital Status and Risk to the Child

The mother's marital status also appears to be a factor in a child's risk of homicide at the hands of the mother. In the Kentucky sample, more single than married mothers had killed their children, and of the single mothers, divorced mothers killed less often than did the mothers who had never married. These patterns speak to two general trends. First, it shows us that economics and family support may, indeed, play a vital role in fatal violence directed at children. Women with little means of support appear to be at the greatest risk of killing their children, because the children may serve as both an inconvenience and an impediment to the women's social and economic development. This does not mean that every unmarried mother, or even a large majority of them, will react violently to her children, but there does appear to be a relationship. Second, women who may not be living with a spouse or partner presently, but have a spouse to whom they have been married in the past, appear to have a decreased risk of killing their children. The reason for this group's decreased risk seems to be financial assistance that may come from the spouse, or the support of the mother's, or even father's, family members (e.g., in-laws, grandparents, etc.).

Age of the Child and Risk of Homicide

The Kentucky data also indicate that a child's risk of murder decreases once he or she reaches the age of 1 year. This finding is validated further by Greenfeld and Snell's (1999) report that mothers are responsible for more child deaths in or near infancy. Thus, the age of greatest vulnerability appears to be in the child's first few years of life. There is another peak of risk after the child grows into the teenage years, when the stresses and demands of parenthood go through many changes. These demands are different from those that appear to put the child at risk in infancy. It may be that the value of the child grows as the child grows older, but it is more likely that the risk of accidental death associated with shaking a child also decreases with age. In any event, as the child begins to move toward adolescence, the conflict between the parent and the child grows as the child begins to express his or her individuality.

FATHERS WHO KILL

Unfortunately, there are many examples of fathers who kill their children. The media is replete with examples, and in any region of the country, one or more of these cases occurs each year. Consider the case of Kayla McKean. In 1998 in central Florida, the father (Richard Adams) became frustrated with his ability to take care of the child and control her incessant crying. In a fit of rage one day when she soiled her pants, Adams threw her against the wall and struck her with a paddle until the 6-year-old stopped breathing. Aided by his wife, Marcie Adams, he took Kayla to Ocala National Forest near Tavares, Florida, where he buried her. It was not until the next morning that Adams called 911 and stated that his daughter was outside playing at their apartment and disappeared. This sequence of events set off a statewide hunt for this child, involving hundreds of volunteers and police officers over a 5-day period. After intense interrogation by police authorities, the stepmother, Marcie Adams, led the police to a shallow grave some 40 miles from their home and confessed to her part of the crime (Schneider, 1998).

Little scholarly attention has been paid to studying the basic etiology of the father who kills his child or children (Ewing, 1997). One of the few was conducted by Campion, Gravens, and Covan (1988). This study found that men who killed their children often shared many common elements with women who killed their children, especially older children. These authors found that many of these men were raised in a very stressful environment. They may have witnessed personal violence between the mother and father, and it is likely that one of their parents either left the house or died. The authors also note that 75% of their sample reported prior psychiatric disorders as children, many had been placed outside of the home for their prior violent aggressive behavior, and many had been both physically and sexually abused as children.

STEPPARENTS WHO KILL

Traditional children's stories usually depict stepmothers as evil. The wicked stepmother is a recurring figure in fairy tales, and stepparents in these stories are not viewed as having the maternal or paternal roles or feelings of biological parents. Real stepparents, of course, are not like those found in fairytales; the vast majority love and care for their stepchildren as best they can, taking on true maternal and paternal feelings and duties. However, the ugly stepparents depicted by children's fiction are not too far removed from reality in a few cases.

Daly and Wilson (1988) report that in almost 15% of the *reported* cases of physical abuse, stepparents are the abusers. These authors estimate that children who are in homes with stepparents are 100 times more likely to be fatally abused than are children who live with both of their biological parents.

Especially disturbing are those cases in which stepfathers physically and/or sexually abuse, and then kill, their stepchildren, while the biological mother denies the existence of the abuse. Such mothers may feel the need to weigh the risks involved to themselves and may feel forced to choose between their children or their mate. For most of us, the choice is obvious: The children always come first. But in a few cases, some women, especially those with low self-esteem, the choice becomes more difficult with age.

Age of the Child and Risk of Homicide by the Stepfather

As is the case with a child's risk of murder by a natural parent, the risk of murder by a stepparent, especially the stepfather, appears to be influenced by the child's age. Data that we gathered from the Crimes Against Children Unit in Louisville, Kentucky show a direct relationship. Very young children (those under the age of 2) are at a greater risk. The risk then drops steadily to about the age of 7, and then rises slowly until the child reaches the age of majority. Even though the risk of victimization rises toward adolescence, it is never as high as it is in infanthood. Reasons for this finding are currently unknown, although anecdotal evidence suggests that many of these killings are unintentional. In many cases, the stepfather is left alone with a crying baby and shakes the child to quiet him or her. Interviews with child killers show this pattern not only with stepparents but also with paternal fathers. Although it is a stretch to say that stepfathers are at increased risk to murder their stepchildren because the children are not their own, every year the media focus attention on a regional case where this type of relationship is present. How this unpublished research compares with other studies and empirical research is currently unknown. Clearly, more research needs to be done in this area.

DISCUSSION AND CONCLUSION

It is difficult for most people to understand those who fatally abuse children. It is important that this chapter and the reader acknowledge that most deaths of children at the hands of their parents are, indeed, unintentional. However, the act and the legal classification and finding of homicide precipitates the inclusion of these cases in this chapter.

In society's attempts to deal with the problems of child abuse and murder, national telephone hotlines have been established. Other innovative approaches, such as the proposal being considered by the legislature of the State of Florida, include setting up centers in hospitals and other community centers where unwanted newborns can be turned over to state officials without fear of legal recourse. This program, although not new, is among the many programs now being explored across the country. The idea is that if the parents know that they can turn over a newborn to the state without being charged with abandonment, it is likely that law enforcement and other officials of the criminal justice system will find fewer children suffocated in plastic bags and dumped in waste repositories.

The family is supposed to be a place of warmth, safety, comfort, and acceptance, but clearly, this is not always the case. The family has become for many the "cradle of violence," where the child is in imminent danger of becoming a murder statistic. As noted above, mothers who kill their children are certainly different from fathers who kill, but knowing these differences does little to help us understand the personalities of parents who intentionally kill their children. We can enumerate certain personality traits— anomie, depression, alcoholism, and so on—but what we need is a better understanding of the total personality of the person who kills and the stresses that can result in the murder of a child. At one time or another, most parents have found themselves in situations where they are at their wit's end and just want their child to be quiet. Why do some stop short of harming their children and others act out of anger and brutalize or even kill their children? We need further empirical and well as qualitative research on these topics, as well as guidance as to what counseling and rehabilitative techniques are effective with parents who have trouble controlling their anger. It is truly interesting that we need to pass a test to drive a car, but we need no education or training to have or raise a child. Granted, it may be legally impossible to mandate that parents cannot have children without receiving some type of educational training, but it is evident that something must be done. It is possible that this issue needs to be addressed by religious groups or organizations before they accept children into the church through a sacrament such as baptism.

NOTE

1. An accident here is not the same as an act of passion. Acts of passion are and can be construed as battery by the parent.

SEX-RELATED HOMICIDE

Sexually motivated homicide is perhaps the most disturbing of all types of murder. These cases, which often involved sexual mutilation of body parts and/or acts of necrophilia, cannibalism, and vampirism, send the terrifying signal that a sexual psychopath is on the loose. These crimes are all too present in the media, especially when they involve children. Witness the case of young Adam Walsh. The 7-year-old boy was abducted from a Hollywood, Florida, shopping center, and his severed head was found 2 weeks later. He was thought to be a victim of a sadistic child offender. Ottis Toole, a sexual sadist and the alleged killing companion of Henry Lucas, confessed to this murder but later recanted. Toole died in prison of a severe medical condition several years ago, and thus the true killer of Adam Walsh is still unknown.

There is probably no one in this country who has not heard of the JonBenet Ramsey case. There have been reports that there was some evidence of sexual activity, although this, too, is an unsolved murder case, and the details are as yet unconfirmed.

Of course, not all of the killings in which sex is a motivating factor involve children or females. In Punta Gorda, Florida, in the summer of 1999, police uncovered the brutalized bodies of six men, called the Hog Trail killings. One victim, William John Melaragno, bore ropelike burns on his body, leading the police to surmise that he had been tied up at one point. The killer stabbed Melaragno stabbed four times, posed his body in the shape of a cross, and then amputated his genitals.

In a 3-year period, six bodies were found by police. One man, Daniel Conahan, was arrested in this case, but he was charged with only one murder, that of Richard Montgomery. APBONLINE reports that Conahan, who is gay, told a former lover that his main sexual fantasy was to "cruise around, pick up hitchhikers or vagrants, take them to the woods, tie them to a tree and 'screw' them" (Heldman, 1999). Conahan lured his victims, who were typically transients, hitchhikers, and hustlers, by promising them money in exchange for having sex and posing for nude bondage shots. Once he had them in a remote area, he gave them alcohol and drugs, thereby incapacitating them. He then tied them to trees. Once he had killed them, he posed their corpses on the ground and often mutilated them. Conahan, who once worked as a nurse, is believed to have disposed of some of the physical evidence (amputated body parts and other evidence) by using hospital biohazard disposal bags. Conahan was convicted of Montgomery's murder and given the death sentence. His case is currently on appeal.

Police files are filled with cases involving homicidal offenders who have made a connection between sexual gratification and sexual violence. The violence in these cases is usually directed against the vulnerable, typically women and children, usually girls. Unless the perpetrator is a homosexual (e.g., Daniel Conahan, Randy Kraft, John Wayne Gacy, Jeffrey Dahmer), males are victims in the minority of cases.

WHAT IS SEXUAL HOMICIDE?

For purposes of this discussion, sexual homicide is defined as murder that combines fatal violence with a sexual element. The violence usually ends with the death of the victim and is often preceded by various aberrant sexual acts. The following story was related to the first author by Jose M., a sexual sadist. Note the elements of the fantasy, the stalk, and, finally, the murder.

Five hours. Five long wretched hours have passed. And still I had not a damn thing to show for the time or the tank full of gas I'd burned up while cruising the highways surrounding my suburban hometown. Off to the west, I could see the sun was already beginning to drop behind the dirty gray hills which lay several miles away. Soon it would be dark outside, and I'd have but little choice but to call it quits for the day. And the thought of this was so infuriating to me that I smashed my fist against the thinly padded surface of the dashboard of my car as if this eruption of pointed violence could somehow exorcise the raging frustration that was threatening to consume me from within. I was feeling threatened. I was feeling betrayed. I felt as if some cruel and unseen power was toying with me, taunting me, deliberately making my life miserable by denying me what I both craved and deserved.

Yet, for all my resolve to crush and destroy, my shoulders were sagging from the weight of disappointment as I gazed off to the west again. Through the side window of my car, I saw that the sun was not completely below the hilly horizon, and I knew in my gut that this day's hunt was doomed to end in failure. It would only be a matter of minutes before twilight was blanketed by darkness. And, from the countless hunting excursions I'd made before this day, I knew all too well that nightfall's arrival had a maddening way of sweeping off the highway all my desired prey, driving them indoors, keeping them impossibly beyond my reach.

Snarling with bitter frustration while switching on my car's headlights, I forced myself to swallow the fact that it was time to call off the hunt. To be sure, I was completely determined to resume my search on the highways tomorrow afternoon, just as soon as I could yank myself away from work. But tonight, I'd have no use for the jagged knife or the two lengths of rope which were tucked, still hidden, inside my jacket. Nor would I get to enjoy any of the novel punishments that I'd been so eager to try out on some low-life wench. Instead I'd be returning to my home completely alone. Empty-handed. Without the prize I was so desperately craving.

And then it happened. Just when I was counting the day a total loss, all of my nerve-endings bounced alive with excitement at what was being illuminated by the bright glare of my headlights. I could hardly believe what I was now seeing on the shoulder of the road some 50 yards in front of me. But there, at long last, I'd found what I'd been searching for throughout the entire afternoon: a lone hitchhiker. Yellow-haired and slender. Unmistakably young. Very definitely female. And there she stood, in the traditional beseeching pose, her thumb jutting toward the sky from the end of her outstretched arm.

Instantly, even before I was braking to slow my car's forward momentum, my decision was made: the small, solitary figure on the roadside was MINE. She didn't know it yet, and it would be perhaps a while before the truth came crashing down upon her. But she now belonged to me. Plain and simple. She was my possession. MY personal property. She was ALL MINE—to do with as I damn well pleased.

"Hi! My name is Becky," the girl said brightly, after swinging open the passenger-side door and ducking her head inside. She was a pretty thing, stylishly dressed, probably no more than 16 or 17. "Can you give me a lift as far as the Oxmoor Mall?"

I was pleasantly surprised by her stated destination. The mall she'd named was very close to where I lived, which would certainly make things a lot easier on me when it came to luring her to my house. "The Oxmoor Mall? Why, I live only a few blocks from there," I answered truthfully, smiling amiably as I spoke. "So I guess you found yourself the right taxi. Hop on inside, little lady! I'll take you all the way there."

Thanking me several times over as she settled into the seat beside me, the small blonde drew the passenger-door shut, and I slowly pulled my car back onto the highway. I'd given her no cause for any alarm, of course, she was completely oblivious to the fact that my hatred and contempt for her was already a rising storm beneath my outward show of friendliness. For, even as I was smiling at her bubbling words of gratitude, my brain was conducting a fast and furious trial inside the privacy of my skull—and SHE was the one and only defendant. I was judging her. And I was condemning her. I was damning this girl named Becky to a fate that would soon have her wishing she'd never been born.

I decided to play some mind games with this young whore to my right, knowing full well that she was still a child. I asked her, "What are you majoring in in college?" I could see her chest swell with some sense of importance that she thought that I thought that she was somewhat older than she really was. She replied, "Well, thank you, but I am 15. I am a sophomore at Jefferson High School." Again I could see her chest swell.

We continued our trek up the I-5 Highway, toward her death, I hoped. I reached inside of my short pocket and retrieved a small, plastic baggy loaded with marijuana. I held it over by the rearview mirror so she was certain to see it. I asked her, "Do you and your friends smoke pot at school?" She looked at me in a skeptical fashion. "You're not a cop, are you?"

I smiled my best smile, white teeth showing, "Hon, I'm anything but a cop. Look in my glove compartment, there's some papers in there."

I looked at my watch, it was 7:20 p.m. I asked her, "What time do you have to be at the mall to meet your friends?"

As she was rummaging through the contents of my compartment, she said it would be about 8 o'clock.

"Oh, you have plenty of time." The bitch has plenty of time to die. She does not know it yet, but the truth will come crashing down on her. The bitch has plenty of time to die.

"Mister, there's no . . ."

I gave her no time to finish her pronouncement. "Oh, geez. That's right. A friend came over to my house last night and we rotated the tires on our cars. I bet he left them on my workbench. Why don't you come home with me?"

In her mind she was conducting her own fast and furious trial. Should she? If she does, she dies. If she doesn't, she lives to see another sunrise. The decision is all hers.

We continue the trek up the I-5 Expressway. I was beginning to feel the gnaw at my stomach. I was hungry for the female meal. It was in this slut's hands if I would feed the meal.

She interrupted my frustration. "At the next exit, there's a 7-11. We can stop there. I'll buy the papers."

In no way was I going to allow myself to pull onto a small parking lot, running the risk that someone might recognize her, myself, my car, or my license number. No. I was not going to run that risk.

Crushed. Devastated. Once again the wiles of the female bitch have defeated me. The ultimate man, the very epitome of masculine power and glory.

I said to her that that was OK, I would just take her on to the mall. We continued the next mile in silence. Finally, in the far distance, I could see the lights of the Oxmoor Mall reflected in the skies. I knew I would have to make my final move or she would be lost to me tonight.

But she said, "If I go to your house, are you sure you can get me to the mall in time to see my friends?"

The bitch was dead. It would be a while, but the bitch was dead.

"Well, Becky, here we are," I announced cheerfully, slowing my car in front of my house and turning onto the driveway. By design, the electrically powered door to my two-car garage was already open. Also, by design, the small control box for the garage-door closing mechanism was tucked inside my jacket pocket, out of my passenger's view. Allowing my car to glide all the way inside my garage, I braked to a stop, then casually turned off the engine and my headlights.

Instantly, it was difficult to see anything beyond one another's shadowy outline. And, before she could suspect that anything was amiss by this sudden darkness, I was reaching inside my jacket and pressing the button on the control box. Noisily, my automatic garage door started clanking down behind us.

At the sound of the lowering door, the little blonde turned her face toward the rear and then back towards me. As I had no further need to respond to her questions and waste words on a continuing charade, I was silent. Instead, I lashed out my right arm with a hard, back-handed motion, plowing my balled-up fist in her stomach. With a loud whooshing sound, the blow knocked all the air out of her lungs, and she doubled over to get her breath. Then, while she struggled to get her breathing muscles working again, I switched on my car's inside light and knelt on the seat beside her crumpled form, a yard-long piece of rope already in my hand. In my heart, I was the scourge of justice to this worthless tramp, so it bothered me not at all to see her clutching and clawing at her midsection in such obvious pain. Indeed, there was something very reassuring about the sight of her agony. It was a good feeling, a heady feeling, an arousing feeling of complete control. Spurred to action by this frame of mind, I grabbed her by the hair and yanked her into a sitting position, snapping her head back over the top of my car seat. Quickly, then, my knife was against her throat, and her mouth opening wide in an effort to let out a scream. Instead of a scream, however, only a strangled gasp could escape past her lips.

"OK, pay attention, slut. If I hear one more sound out of you, or if you make even one false move, you're gonna be dead real quick. And I mean exactly what I say. Do you get that loud and clear?"

As best she could with my hand still gripping her hair, my little captive nodded her head up and down just as I expected she would. I pulled out two lengthy pieces of cloth from beneath my seat, using them to cover her eyes and mouth. When they were tied securely, I let her sit unmolested for a few minutes while I smoked a cigarette. Finally, when I finished my cigarette, I flicked off the inside light and pushed open the door of my car. After grabbing her by the arm, I pulled the bitch toward me, hauling her across my seat onto the floor of my garage. Although she was whimpering and trembling very noticeably, she made no attempt to struggle as I lifted her up and helped her onto her feet. I placed my knife again at her throat and I said, "Remember one false move and you're gonna be dead." Again she nodded her head up and down the best she could with my left hand holding her hair in such a fashion. This nod was all she could do in the face of male superiority. After all, I AM the ULTIMATE MAN!

I looked over my right shoulder toward the door which would lead down a hallway past my kitchen and into the bedroom where everything was ready for little Ms. Becky. Then all hell broke loose. The bitch ran from me. Despite being blindfolded and hobbled, the bitch ran from me. She ran into the lowered garage door, fell onto her back, and with her bound feet started kicking at the door, making a terrible din. The neighbors were going to hear, I thought. They would call the police! I would get caught! I stood there, my feet seemingly implanted in concrete. Finally my brain announced: Dammit, do something! Get her!

I ran toward her, but I tripped over my feet. The knife I was holding fell from my hand and slid under the car. In the murky darkness of my garage, I searched for the unseen knife. All the while she was making the terrible and loud noises. Finally realizing that I would find the knife in time, I got up and ran toward her as she, too, was getting up. With my low-ered right shoulder, I ran into the small of her back and sent her crashing onto a pile of weightlifting equipment that was mounted in the corner of my garage. A dumb bell, a bar bell, something fell upon her neck, making an awful, crunching sound. I lifted this worthless piece of female meat over my shoulder and marched down the hall. Reaching my bedroom I dumped and locked her inside my closet door with a sliding bolt mounted on the outside, then hurried back to my living room, where I peered nervously through the windows. All was quiet in front of my house. I knew in my gut that everything was going to be just fine.

And everything was ready for my little Miss Becky. Indeed, every-thing had been set up and laid out since mid-afternoon, when my gut had loudly informed me that this was the day to take up the righteous hunt. Propped against one wall, there was a huge, full-length mirror, where the young wench would watch her own reflection as she stripped away by her own hand all the skin-tight harlot's clothing that she wore and showed off so proudly. And, snaking onto the mattress from the four corners of the bed, there were individual ropes, one for each wrist and ankle, which would stretch her out and hold her down while she received her just desserts. Then, on a low wooden table next to my bed, there rested some of the tools that would assist in her punishment: an assorted collection of heavy leather belts; large pieces of rough-grit sandpaper; a plastic box of jagged-tooth metal clips; a bare, scorching-hot lamp bulb attached to a small, handheld lamp; and, as an added twist, a small container of mace—the very same stuff that females so often love to spray in the face of their male superiors.

Yes, all of this was ready and waiting for my little captive, and I was seething with anticipation, my temples pounding with excitement, as I pulled back the sliding bolt on the outside of my closet. Slowly, then, I started inching open the door, my fist raised to deliver still another blow to her stomach if she was stupid enough to resist me yet again. And when I saw that her legs were still extended flat upon the closet floor, I threw the door wide open, almost howling out loud from my eagerness get my hands on this little bitch.

Suddenly, then, I froze where I stood, sensing immediately that something was terribly, terribly wrong. For, instead of reacting to the sound of my presence, the small blonde remained slumped over to one side, looking like a broken doll, her head sagging motionless against her breast. Her skin was an unnatural pasty-white color and several drops of blood stained the snug material on her thigh. She was perfectly still, much too still, her body exhibiting not even a twitch or a flicker of movement. Then, at last, I noticed the swelling and dark discoloration on the front of her neck, and I remembered the sickening, crunching sound I had heard in my garage. And, almost at once, I realized that her throat had been crushed on my weight pile and she would never move another muscle on her own again. She was dead.

As the reality of this sank quickly into my brain, my mind just seemed to snap in two, and I exploded into a violent rage. Savagely, I yanked the whore out of my closet by her hair and threw her body onto my bed, where I ripped all her clothes in tattered shreds. Then, everything took on the quality of a frenetic but disjointed dream as I was beating her with my fists this moment, whipping her with a leather strap the next, and then stomping her with my feet the moment after that, seemingly with no transition in between. I was utterly beyond control, snarling like a rabid animal, attacking with all the fury of a madman. And as I continued to batter the harlot's naked corpse, I became more and more enraged that she would not thrash in agony beneath my frenzied blows, that she would not fill my bedroom with the sound of anguished female screams. Yet I could not stop and face my demons of despair. So I hit and whipped her and kicked her again and again, as if I could somehow smash my way into the world of the dead and make her suffer still.

Once again I had been tricked and fallen victim to a harlot's treachery. So despite all the difficulties of a night time hunt, I made up my mind to get back onto the highway without delay. The evening was still young, anything was possible.

The minutes passed until they tallied more than an hour. And, once again, I was smiling as I pulled my car onto the driveway for the second time that evening. Pressing gently on the brake pedal, I rolled to a complete stop inside my open garage, then nonchalantly switched off my ignition and headlights. Instantly, everything was very dark, and I reached inside my jacket to depress the button on a small, rectangular plastic box. Right on cue, my garage door began lowering automatically, and I felt a familiar twist of sudden movement from the passenger seat to my right.

"Hey! What are you doing?" cried a youthful feminine voice. And, just as this shrill voice went silent, my garage door slammed with a boom.

I had not returned empty-handed. And the night indeed would be redeemed.

This particular crime reflects several elements of sexual homicide: the killer's fantasy, the controlled conversation, and, finally, the murder. All indicate the killer's needs as well as his desires. The fantasies in this story are not all that unusual for sexually motivated killing. Consider the case of Daniel Rakowitz, age 28, who was arrested for the murder of Monika Beerle, a former girlfriend. Beerle's remains had been reduced so that they fit into a five-gallon bucket, which was found in the baggage claim area of the Port Authority bus terminal in New York City. Police alleged that Rakowitz, a former short-order cook, stabbed Beerle to death when she threatened to leave him, then boiled her body parts to separate flesh from bones and flushed the skin down the toilet. An anthropophagist, Rakowitz, like Edward Gein, Jeffrey Dahmer, Albert Fish, and others, possessed a desire to eat body parts for sexual stimulation. This consumption of human flesh is accompanied by a sense of eroticism and, finally, sexual gratification.

Myron Lance and Walter Kelbach are two more examples of sexual killers. Their victims were all young males who were taken into secluded areas and killed. According to their psychologist, Kelbach spoke of the enjoyment he received when he cut into the flesh of the victims: "It was like cutting foam rubber . . . and the veins sliced like boiled spaghetti" (A. Carlisle, personal communication, March 28, 1991). Such statements are typical of those made by people who commit sexual homicide.

ELEMENTS IN SEXUAL HOMICIDE

From the perspective of those who have been involved in the criminal justice system and have talked with sexual offenders and seen their handiwork, there are certain elements in these offenders' sexual lifestyles that are also found in "normal" people. However, exactly what separates the offenders from the "normal" population is unknown. Regardless, it does appear that those who commit sexual homicide have little control over their propensities for sexual violence, nor do they wish for it. Let us now examine those elements.

Fantasy

Everyone has a sexual fantasy, and probably more than one. Many people's sexual fantasies often center on romance, love, caring, and touching. But for the sexual sadist who is involved in sexual homicide, sexual fantasies contain violent scripts for action. Bondage, mutilation, and other acts of sadism are part of the scenario. The story related earlier by Jose M. contains typical elements of a fantasy script. The manner in which the bed was laid out, with "the four ropes snaking from each corner," the full-length mirror, the can of mace, and even the latch on the *outside* of the closet door—all reflect the killer's fantasy.

More than one killer has mentioned the role of the sexual fantasy in the acts that led up to their victims' deaths (e.g., see Holmes & Holmes, 1998; McGuire & Norton, 1988; Michaud & Aynesworth, 1983; Ressler, Burgess, & Douglas, 1988). In addition to the elements of fantasy already mentioned, the killer's scenario may include such acts as vampirism, cannibalism, necrophilia, picquerism, lust murder, and flagellation.

Symbolism

Sex and sexuality are very visible in our society. In the world of advertising, sex is used to sell everything from automobiles to computers and from dishwashing detergent to breakfast cereal. Ads that include sexually attractive models enhance product sales—Madison Avenue has known this for years.

There are two types of symbolism in sex: fetishes and partialisms. A fetish is an object to which sex has been visually attached. There are many examples of fetishes, such as shoes, stockings, and underwear. Certainly, the average man on the street has at least one fetish. One has only to look at pornography to see fetishes popular in our country today. Jerry Brudos, a lust killer currently in prison in Oregon, is a shoe fetishist. At times, he forced his wife to wear shoes that he had stolen from other women (Stack, 1983). In interviews, Jose, whose story appeared earlier, denied a particular fondness for any material object. However, he did say that he liked the "cheerleader" type; this kind of image served as a visual aphrodisiac for this lust killer.

A partialism is a part of the body to which people have attached sexual significance. Breasts, buttocks, and legs are common partialisms for men in the United States. Buttocks appear to be the most popular partialism for women in the United States (Holmes, 1991). When an individual needs a fetish or a partialism in order to perform sexually, that person is said to have a paraphilia or "perversion."

Sometimes, serial killers will favor victims with a particular partialism in common. Once this is determined, such information can be helpful to investigators. However, it is important that any information given to the public on this subject be accurate. For example, one author stated that Ted Bundy killed women with long, dark hair parted in the middle. This information became part of the profile that police used to link various murder cases from 1974 to 1978. However, Bundy was not exclusive. Among his victims were Susan Rancourt, who had blonde hair, and Laura Aime, who was a redhead. Kimberly Leach, his last known victim, had short brown hair. But law enforcement leaped upon this simplistic presumption, and women without this partialism felt safe from the "Ted Killer." In effect, this misinformation increased the danger for many women of being victimized by Bundy. Women who did not possess the stated partialism felt quite safe from him and thus were less wary and more vulnerable.

Jose mentions early in his letter about the partialisms that attract him: blonde hair, blue eyes, and unmistakably young. He mentioned during an interview that he was not consciously aware of selecting victims who met this description. Only after several years of reflection in prison did he become aware of the sexual symbolisms involved in his victim selection process.

Ritualism

If something works well in a person's sexual life, he or she will usually continue to practice that rewarding act. It is the same for sexual sadists, who will continue to torture and kill until they tire of the "routine." At that point, they may alter slightly the ways in which they select, torture, kill, and dispose of their victims.

Ritualism is present in many human interactions, both sexual and nonsexual. Following a ritual of sorts becomes part of any couple's sexual habits. Interacting in ritualized ways is part of the process of living together.

In sexual sadism, the perpetrator feels the need to repeat his crimes in the same or similar fashion. This is particularly true of a killer's early crimes. One killer told the first author in an interview that he made his victims repeat aloud some of the material he had read in a book of pornography that he found in his father's garage when he was 9 years old (this serial killer began his lust killings when he was 18). If the victims did not repeat the words as they were instructed, he killed them quickly. If they cooperated, the kill was prolonged until the complete script (the ritual) was fulfilled.

Compulsion

In interviews with sexual sadists, we have found compulsion to be an integral part of the conversation. This is the sole common element we have found in all the sexual murderers we have studied personally. One killer spoke of the "awful, craving, eating feeling" that became evident when a long time had passed since the last kill. Indeed, Jose said, "I woke up one morning knowing I was going to kill like I had killed many mornings before." He then remarked, "Killing was the only way for me to placate this feeling." Another sadist called this feeling a "beast," another called it the "entity," and yet another called it the "shadow." Regardless of the name, it is the common element in sexual sadists' personalities.

This feeling of compulsion may overtake the traditional manner in which a murderer kills. It may also alter his ideal victim type. One man interviewed by the first author said,

> I drove downtown to pick up a victim. I had not killed in more than a month, and the pit in my stomach announced that the hunt was on. As I drove down Main Street, I saw her. Blonde, young, good body. I waited for the light to turn green, but before it did, she got into a car with another man. The knot in my stomach was churning so bad that I announced to myself that the next woman I saw would be mine. The next woman was two 12-year-old girls. I would not have selected them as my victims had not the signal been so strong inside of me.

All people have some feelings of sexual compulsion, and this feeling certainly has an impact on sexual behavior. However, when a person can achieve sexual gratification only when the selected partner (victim) does as commanded, compulsion moves into the area of paraphilia.

LUST MURDER

Vernon Geberth (1991) makes a distinction between lust murder and sex-related homicide. A former commander of the New York Police Department and a dynamic speaker, he has traveled across this country offering seminars on homicide and sex crimes. In his presentations, Geberth defines the lust murder as one typified by a gross sexual assault involving deep personality pathology and including body mutilations and displacement of selected body parts (partialisms) that have sexual significance to the killer.

Although the lust killing is one type of sexual homicide, the lust killer as a sexual psychopath possesses certain distinct characteristics. The psychopath, or sociopath, has received a great deal of attention. Conklin (1989) defines a psychopath as "an asocial, aggressive, and highly impulsive person who feels little or no guilt for this antisocial behavior and who is unable to form lasting bonds of affection with other people" (p. 164). Rush (1991) offers a more comprehensive definition: a person who is not insane but who has a severe mental or personality disorder. According to Rush, the psychopath is deficient in the capacity to feel guilt, accept love, and empathize with others (Rush, 1991, p. 255).

The true psychopath is one who has been thwarted in the development of his personality. This results in a set of behaviors that is aimed at self-fulfillment, even at the expense of the needs or safety of another. Psychopaths may come from various backgrounds, but often, these individuals will come into contact with the criminal justice system at some time in their lives because of their reluctance to abide by the rules and regulations of society. It is useful to view psychopathy as a continuum. Few psychopaths operate on a level that is completely unconcerned with the thoughts, feelings, and actions of others; some who are diagnosed as psychopathic show some concern, at least on a superficial level, for the people with whom they come into contact. However, when the psychopathic personality becomes involved in sexual homicide, the crimes are often bizarre in content, with acts of mutilation, necrophilia, and so on.

CHARACTERISTICS OF THE PSYCHOPATH

* Superficial charm and good intelligence
* Absence of delusions and other signs of irrational thinking
* Absence of nervousness or psychoneurotic manifestations
* Unreliability
* Untruthfulness and insincerity
* Lack of remorse or shame
* Inadequately motivated antisocial behavior
* Poor judgment and failure to learn by experience
* Pathologic egocentricity and incapacity for love
* General poverty in major affective reactions
* Specific loss of insight
* Unresponsiveness in general interpersonal relations
* Fantastic and uninviting behavior with and without drink
* Suicide rarely carried out
* Sex life impersonal, trivial, and poorly integrated
* Failure to follow any life plan

SOURCE: Cleckley, H. (1982). *Mask of Sanity.* New York: Plume.

The Lust Murderer

The Federal Bureau of Investigation has taken the lead in developing a typology of lust murderers. From an investigation of 36 incarcerated offenders (none of whom is identified by name), two polar types of lust murderers were developed: *organized* and *disorganized*. The organized lust murderer tends to be a loner because he wants to be, because he feels other are unworthy of this friendship; he is a loner by choice, and the *nonsocial* label (which has now been dropped by the FBI) signified this. On the other hand, the *asocial* label signified that the disorganized offender tends to be a loner because others are reluctant to become personally involved with him, feeling that he is somehow strange or bizarre.

The disorganized lust killer is disorganized in his total behavior; his work, home, vehicle, clothing, demeanor, and so on all reflect this state. The disorganized offender is typically low in intelligence, socially inadequate, alone, and low in birth order status (that is, he is not usually the oldest or the middle child in his family of origin). He usually lives and works near his crime zone. Research suggests that the disorganized offender is often a nonathletic white male with an introverted personality (Ressler et al., 1988).

Disorganized offenders also tend to share several postoffense behaviors. They often return to the scenes of their crimes, and they sometimes even place "in memoriam" personal ads about their victims in local newspapers. These offenders also may change residences (but usually within the same neighborhood) as well as jobs after they kill ("The Men Who Murdered," 1985).

The disorganized offender does not plan his attacks, if for no other reason than lack of ability to do so. He does not usually use restraints on the victim, mostly because the attacks are spontaneous and unplanned, and the victim is simply an object for the use of pointed violence. Often, this kind of offender finds victims in the area where both he and the victim live and/or work, at least in part because this killer feels comfortable only in areas with which he is familiar ("The Men Who Murdered," 1985).

The disorganized offender often disfigures the faces of his victims. He also often mutilates victims' bodies, removing sexual parts and taking these parts with him from the crime scene. Furthermore, his victims' bodies show evidence of a great amount of overkill. There may be object penetration and evidence of necrophilia.

The crime scene of the disorganized asocial offender is usually quite chaotic, yielding a great deal of physical evidence. This offender does not appear to be nearly as concerned as the organized offender about avoiding detection.

The organized nonsocial murderer is the theoretical opposite of the disorganized offender. Such exact oppositions seldom exist in reality, but the overall typology is an important starting point for an examination not only of the offenders themselves but also of the crime scenes they leave behind.

The organized offender is neat and organized in everything he does. This offender's workplace, home, car, and personal appearance all reflect the need for order, cleanliness, and neatness. The organized offender may be said to be an anal-retentive personality type; there is a place for everything

---

CRIME SCENE TRAITS

- ✦ Spontaneous offense
- ✦ Victim/location known
- ✦ Victim depersonalized
- ✦ Minimal conversation
- ✦ Crime scene random and sloppy
- ✦ Sudden violence to the victim
- ✦ Minimal use of restraints
- ✦ Sexual acts after death
- ✦ Body left in view
- ✦ Evidence/weapon often present
- ✦ Body left at the scene

SOURCE: "The Men Who Murdered" (1985).

---

and everything must be in its place. This offender is nonsocial because he chooses to be. In everyday life, this offender believes that no one is good enough for him to risk friendship; with friendship, he risks vulnerability.

The FBI suggests that there may be precipitating factors in organized lust murders. Stress may trigger a killing, but because of the perpetrator's organized personality, he can delay the kill itself. For example, one lust killer currently in prison in a western state told the first author in a interview that he killed one young woman because she dared to look at another man while she was out on a date with him. This was enough for him to go into an emo tional tirade that resulted in her death. Her murder was accompanied by sadistic sexual torture and dismemberment. At first glance, this may seem like the work of a disorganized killer, but further examination shows that although the external stressor was the motivation for the murder, the killer still behaved in an organized fashion. He took the victim to his comfort zone, involved himself in a process kill, and then disposed of the body.

Other personal traits of the organized offender include high intelligence, social adeptness, and relative ease in adjusting to new situations. Many organized offenders appear to have normal sex lives; often, they have spouses or live-in partners. These offenders tend to be both occupationally

CRIME SCENE TRAITS OF THE ORGANIZED LUST KILLER

- ◆ Planned offense
- ◆ Targeted stranger
- ◆ Personalized victim
- ◆ Controlled conversation
- ◆ Controlled crime scene
- ◆ Submissive victim
- ◆ Aggressive acts
- ◆ Restraints used
- ◆ Body moved
- ◆ Weapon taken
- ◆ Little physical evidence

SOURCE: "The Men Who Murdered" (1985).

and spatially mobile, and they usually have no particular need to stay in familiar areas ("The Men Who Murdered," 1985).

The organized offender who is a true psychopath has little trouble making friends, but he keeps all friendships on a superficial level. Ted Bundy's ability to charm is an excellent example. In an interview, the first author found that Bundy was so capable of putting a person at ease that after 5 minutes it seemed as if he had known this serial killer for years. This is one reason why these murderers are so effective.

The organized offender, according to the research of the FBI, not only commits the crime in a fashion much different from that of the disorganized killer but also behaves differently after the crime is committed. For example, the organized killer often moves the body from the kill site to a disposal site. He may sexually mutilate and dismember the body and/or perform a variety of other sexual aberrations.

Sex-related homicide can involve an interesting blend of various levels of sexual behaviors. The lust killer may be involved in more than simply aberrant acts and practices; he may have an added propensity for sadism and violence, and for such acts as anthropophagy, necrophilia, erotic asphyxiation, and picquerism. In addition, elements of pyromania and infibulation are sometimes present. Crimes of sexual violence are often connected with many of these paraphilias.

GLOSSARY OF SEXUAL PARAPHILIAS

Anilingus	Oral stimulation of the anus
Anthropophagy	Sexual gratification from cannibalism
Bestiality	Sexual gratification with an animal
Coprophilia	Sexual gratification associated with handling, eating, or smelling excrement
Coprolagnia	Sexual gratification associated with using sexually oriented words
Cunnilingus	Oral stimulation of the vagina, vulva, or clitoris
Exhibitionism	Sexual gratification associated with exposing one's genitals in an inappropriate situation
Fellatio	Oral stimulation of the penis
Flagellation	Sexual gratification from whipping or being whipped
Frottage	Sexual stimulation from rubbing up against another person; the victim is not a willing participant
Gerontophilia	Sexual preference for older people
Infibulation	Sexual stimulation from the torture of one's own genitals
Kleptomania	Sexual stimulation from shoplifting
Lust murder	Sexually motivated homicide, often accompanied by sexual mutilation
Masochism	Sexual gratification from self-inflicting mental or physical pain

GLOSSARY *(continued)*

Necrophilia	Sexual gratification from corpses
Osphresiophilia	Sexual gratification or excitement from odors
Picquerism	Sexual stimulation from stabbing, cutting, or wounding flesh
Pygmalionism	Sexual stimulation from statues, dolls, or mannequins
Pyromania	Sexual stimulation from fire setting
Rape	Sexual intercourse with another person without his or her consent
Sadism	Sexual stimulation from inflicting mental or physical pain on another person
Sodomy	Sexual penetration of any artificial orifice
Transsexual	A person who is biologically one sex and psychologically the other sex
Transvestite	A cross-dresser, usually a heterosexual male
Tribadism	Sexual gratification of one woman from rubbing up against the pubic area of another woman; also, one who uses a dildo
Triolism	Sexual gratification associated with seeing oneself or another in sexual acts (e.g., use of self-made video, instant cameras, etc.)
Voyeurism	Sexual excitement from seeing others in private scenes, usually sexual scenes
Zoophilia	Sexual excitement associated with handling, feeling, or kissing animals; does not include bestiality

Anthropophagy

Anthropophagists receive sexual gratification from eating the flesh (more commonly called cannibalism) or drinking the blood (more commonly called vampirism) of a victim (Holmes, 1991, p. 116). Jeffrey Dahmer was a notable example. In the second author's files, there was a recent case in Florida where an engineer had killed eight women, kept their blood in his refrigerator, and drank it when the compulsion to do so became strong.

It is unclear at this point what leads individuals to find sexual gratification in eating flesh or drinking blood. What is clear is that those who have begun these practices will tend to continue them.

Necrophilia

Perhaps one of the most bizarre sexual practices is necrophilia, or sexual intercourse with the dead. Necrophilia is a predominantly male sexual paraphilia, but a few female necrophiliacs have been noted in the professional literature (see Ellis, 1986; Freire, 1981). Douglas Clark, the Hollywood Strip Killer, decapitated at least one of his female victims and used the head in sexual acts (Farr, 1992).

Necrophilia is not as rare in sex-related homicides as was once thought (Bartholomew, Milte, & Galbally, 1978; Brill, 1941; Burg, 1992). Again, Ted Bundy provides an example. He kept one victim, a young woman from Utah, for 9 days after he killed her. He stated in an interview with the first author that he kept her under his bed, in his closet, and on his bed. After all, he said, there was no rush to remove the body because he knew no one would be coming to his apartment. He sexually assaulted her for 8 days after he had killed her. Another serial killer, Jerry Brudos, admitted to having sexually assaulted two of his four known victims after they were dead (Rule, 1988).

Necrophilia consists of three levels, the first of which involves only the fantasy. At this level, sexual pleasure is gained from pretending that one's sexual partner is dead at the time of sexual activity; there is no wish to actually have a sexual encounter with a dead body. This type of fantasy is fairly common among some men who frequent prostitutes. One prostitute told the first author about two of her customers who pay her to pretend to be dead, one a university dean and the other an attorney. One of the men wanted only to look at her as she lay completely still on the bed. He would then masturbate (Holmes, 1991, p. 59).

The second level of necrophilia is someone who has a sexual relationship with someone who is already dead. This type of paraphiliac will often deliberately position himself in work situations that allow access to dead bodies (e.g., funeral homes or morgues). According to Ressler et al. (1988), this type of person usually is classifiable as a disorganized offender.

The third level of necrophilia, and clearly the most dangerous, is the necrosadistic offender. This person kills so that he can have sex with a dead body. As Money (1984) notes, the act of sadistic necrophilia must be viewed as the ultimate and most extreme form of erotic eligibility distancing. Rosman and Resnick (1989) note that only a few necrophiliacs are necrosadistic; most will simply take advantage of situations where they have ready access to dead bodies.

No one knows the exact cause of necrophilia. By examining the fantasies, however, Calef and Weinshel (1972) and Faguet (1980) offer a psychodynamic explanation: The offender wants to return to the maternal body. Others believe that necrophiliacs are feebleminded (Ellis, 1946) or possess gross personality defects (Katchadourian & Lunde, 1975). What is certain is that the victim is dead and can offer no resistance to the sexual abuse of the perpetrator (Holmes, 1991; Weeks, 1986).

Pyromania

Pyromania is eroticized fire setting. It is a pathological condition characterized by a sense of psychological compulsion that the offender has a great deal of difficulty containing. Of course, not all cases of fire setting involve pyromaniacs. Some fires are set for insurance purposes, some for business recovery purposes, and others as a means of revenge. It is eroticized fire setting that is the focus of this section.

Masters and Robertson (1990), for example, stated that they have found that as many as 40% of all set fires are caused by pyromaniacs. This estimate may be too high, but unfortunately, there is no way we can currently validate this statistic.

Pyromaniacs set fires from a feeling of sexual compulsion. There is an erotic component to the fire-setting act itself, and the pyromaniac becomes sexually aroused, even to the point of involuntary orgasm, while watching a fire he has set and all the commotion that surrounds the firefighters and the flames.

It is unknown what launches a person into compulsive and erotic fire setting. Bourget and Bradford (1987) believe that some type of situational cause initiates the action. They recount the story of a young adult arrested for a series of fire settings. When his social history was taken, he was found to have been greatly interested in fires as a child, but that he did not start his first fire until he was an adult. He had been rejected by women he attempted to meet at a local bar, and in a fit of rage, he set fire to the bar. This was his first in a series of fires. He connected a sexual component with the need to set a fire. When he believed he was rejected by a young woman, he set a fire. He fantasized about the women in the crowd who were watching the fire and became sexually aroused. He usually left the scene in order to masturbate. Later, a sense of power became a part of the eroticized fire-setting scenario. Money (1984) reports a similar case in his study of pyromaniacs.

Obviously, pyromania is a very dangerous sex crime that often results in the death of innocent people. Great care must be taken in the detection and treatment of those involved in this crime. Unfortunately, too little is known about the etiology and the treatment perspectives of this form of sex offender; it is clear that more research needs to be done.

CONCLUSION

This chapter has focused on dangerous sex crimes that too often result in death. In some cases, the victims of these crimes are carefully selected; in others, they just happen to be in the wrong place at the wrong time. We have addressed the victim selection process, the role of fantasy, and the commission of the homicide. In all instances mentioned in this chapter, sex plays an integral role in the crimes discussed. The type of sexual paraphilia will vary, obviously, from some forms of sadism to the more bizarre types of sexual activities, such as necrophilia and pyromania.

MURDER IN THE WORKPLACE

In March 1995, Christopher Green, a former postal worker, killed two former coworkers and two customers. Green said that he was trying to hold up the post office because he was deeply in debt.

In April 1995, James Daniel Simpson, a former refinery worker, walked into his company's plant, where he killed his former boss, his boss's wife, and three former coworkers. Simpson then shot himself. He died later that day.

A former San Diego State University graduate student, Frederick Martin Davidson, killed three engineering university faculty members who were also members of his thesis committee. Davidson stated that he believed all three members of his committee were conspiring to keep him from securing a good job. He received three life sentences.

The data from the National Crime Victimization Surveys (NCVS) for 1992-1996 indicate that there were more than 2 million violent victimizations in the workplace (Bureau of Justice Statistics, 1998). Needless to say, workplace violence is an emerging problem that results in great suffering and deaths. The survey data also report additional, disturbing statistics:

- More than 1,000 workplace deaths occurred annually.

- The most common type of workplace victimization was simple assault, with an estimated 1.5 million assaults occurring each year. U.S. residents also suffered 51,000 rapes and other sexual assaults and about 84,000 robberies while they were at work.

- Annually, more than 230,000 police officers became victims of a nonfatal violent crime while they were on duty.

- About 40% of victims of nonfatal violence in the workplace reported that they knew their offenders.

- Women were more likely than men to be victimized by someone they knew.

- Approximately 12% of the nonfatal violent workplace crimes resulted in an injury to the victim. Of those injured, about half received medical treatment.

- Intimates (current and former spouses, boyfriends, and girlfriends) were identified by the victims as the perpetrators of about 1% of all workplace violent crime.

Workplace violence occurs in various settings. For example, David Burke was terminated from Pacific Southwest Airlines. Angry, he boarded a PSA plane, following his ex-boss. As the plane was airborne, Burke shot and killed his boss, causing the airplane to crash. Forty-three people on board, including Burke, were killed. In Mississippi, Kenneth Tornes, a firefighter, returned to his firehouse one evening. He killed four supervisors before he was wounded in a gunfight with the police. In California, Willie Woods, a Los Angeles electrician, went to his workplace and shot and killed two supervisors and two fellow employees. He was arrested at the crime scene by two police officers who happened to be in the area. On April 3, 1995, James Simpson walked into the oil refinery where he once worked and killed his former boss, his boss's wife, and three other employees. He then shot himself.

There are other disgruntled employees who kill. Witness the case of Joseph Harris, 35. A former postal worker, Harris had a reputation of simply disliking people. His coworkers stated that it did not make any difference if someone was male or female, black or white, Harris disliked everyone. He was fired for refusing to cooperate with a "fitness for duty" psychological exam ordered for him by his former supervisor, Carol Ott.

One night, Harris went to Ott's home dressed in a bulletproof vest and armed with two submachine guns, grenades, and a sword. He slashed her to death and shot and killed her fiancé, Cornelius Kasten, Jr. He then walked in the back door of the post office in Ridgewood, New Jersey, using a key that was given to mail sorters, his former job. He killed two employees. Harris hid from police in the post office for almost 5 hours before finally surrendering. He had left a note at his home that contained information illustrating his dissatisfaction with the post office. He believed that he had not been treated fairly, and he used his act of mass murder to express his anger.

More than 30 years ago, Robert Earl Mack was fired from his job at General Dynamics, a defense contractor. Mack was 42 years old and had worked for the company for the past 25 years. In the previous year, fellow employees had noted a change in Mack's work habits and personality. He began to show up late and then miss days of work. Nine days after Mack was fired, he was scheduled to appear before an appeals board. During a break in the meeting, Mack opened fire and shot and killed his former coworkers. He then surrendered to the local authorities.

CHAPTER 9

TRAITS OF THE DISGRUNTLED EMPLOYEE MASS KILLER

Violence committed in the workplace usually takes one of three forms:

- The violence is committed by people who work or used to work in the company where the crime occurred.

- The violence is committed by someone who is or was a customer of the company where the crime occurred.

- The violence is committed by people who have no relationship with the company.

In examining these three forms of mass murder in the workplace, it is apparent that many of these crimes are committed by people who have a relationship with the company (Seger, 1993). One, Frederick Davidson, killed three members of his thesis committee. At first glance, this may not appear to fit the traits or characteristics of a disgruntled employee mass killer. However, upon closer examination, a case can be made that this killer was a "customer" of the university, and Davidson was to receive a product, a degree. He believed that the university was negligent in not assisting him in his employment endeavors as well as delaying granting him his degree.

Other cases are more clear. Joseph Harris, for example, went into his place of former employment, a post office, and killed four coworkers. Joseph Wesbecker did the same when he returned to the Standard Gravure Printing Company looking for supervisors who were, in Wesbecker's mind, responsible for his disability leave.

The disgruntled employee mass killer has certain traits that are fundamentally different from the other types of mass killers, as we show in the next sections.

Motivation

The motivation to kill comes from within the mind of the killer (O'Boyle, 1992; Roth, 1994). There are no motivations that arise from outside the personality of the offender. Witness again the case of Joseph Harris. He was often belittled by his coworkers (Losey, 1994). The blame for all of his problems rested outside his own arena of responsibility. The motivation to kill, however, rested within his personality.

Anticipated Gain

The disgruntled employee expects some reward, either expressive or psychological, for his act of mass murder, and this is hard for most people to understand. How could killing innocent people, many of whom were workplace associates, be a psychologically pleasurable thing? But for the disgruntled employee, the answer to this question is easy to address. From one episodic act of homicide, attention is called to both the person committing the act and the occurrences that brought about the killings. Of course, these occurrences are in the mind of the killer (intrinsic motivation), but they add substance to the motivation and draw attention to his perceived injustices. Maybe this is a rationalization for the killings, a denial of injury, a denial of victims, and a denial of responsibility (Sykes & Matza, 1957).

Victim Selectivity

The victims are often former coworkers of the killer. In the case of Joseph Harris, the two employees and the former supervisor came into contact with him almost daily. As a mail sorter for the post office, he interacted daily with other workers despite his abrasive attitude and personality. When

TABLE 9.1 Selected Disgruntled Employee Mass Killers or Suspected Killers

Name	State	Victims
David Burke	California	Killed 43 people in an airplane
Frederick Davidson	California	Killed 3 members of his thesis committee
Gian Ferri	California	Killed 6 people in his attorney's office
Christopher Green	California	Killed 4 people at a post office
Willie Woods	California	Killed 4 coworkers
Eric Houston	California	Killed 4 people at his former high school
Matthew Beck	Connecticut	Killed 4 coworkers
Richard Herr	Delaware	Killed 3 coworkers
Clifton McCree	Florida	Killed 5 fellow workers
Joseph Wesbecker	Kentucky	Shot 7 people at his workplace
Kenneth Jones	Mississippi	Killed wife and four coworkers
Kenneth Tornes	Mississippi	Killed spouse and 4 coworkers
Joseph Harris	New Jersey	Killed 4 people at a post office
James Davis	North Carolina	Killed 3 coworkers
Gerald Clemons	Ohio	Killed 3 people at his former workplace
James Simpson	Texas	Killed boss, boss's wife, and 3 coworkers
Michael Barton	Georgia	Killed wife, two children, and 7 people at work

he killed his victims at the post office, those workers were, unfortunately, at the wrong place at the wrong time. Thus, victims are selected on a random basis.

There needs to be a clarification regarding the randomness of victim selection. True, the victims are often coworkers or former coworkers. But when this mass killer enters the place of employment, the victims are selected usually because they are right in front of him. The disgruntled employee mass killer may enter the facility seeking a specific target, such as a former supervisor, but others are killed with no predetermined selection process. The perpetration of fatal violence is directed toward those people in the workplace who are working that day (Bensimon, 1994).

Victim Relationship

The victims of the disgruntled employee are typically not related to the killer by either blood or marriage. The only ties (not relationships) are those that they all share by working in the same facility, be it a post office, factory, or office building.

As noted in the case study later in this chapter, Joseph Wesbecker had been employed by the same company for more than 20 years. Certainly, he knew some of the people with whom he worked during those years. However, all admitted that they had never been to Wesbecker's home, and none knew this killer on a personal level. He was only a fellow employee. They all suspected Wesbecker was strange, and they felt that his behavior bordered on the weird. None admitted to having personal ties with this man. Wesbecker fits the profile of the disgruntled employee type. A loner who was on medication for his mental illness, had an inordinate interest in weapons, and held a grudge against the administrators of his former employment for his involuntary separation from work, Wesbecker ended his own life and prevented further investigation into his mind and pathology to seek answers to important questions.

Spatial Mobility

The disgruntled employee is typically a geographically stable mass killer. He has roots in the community—his family, his worship center, his recreation, and his employment. He works for a long period of time in his place of employment, but over time, he builds up a sense of anomie, hate, and revenge. Eventually, he acts out this rage. Table 9.2 contains information regarding the various phases of violence in the workplace where the disgruntled employee will react.

TABLE 9.2   Levels of Personal Violence in the Workplace

Level 1

- Refuses to cooperate with immediate supervisor
- Spreads rumors and gossip to harm others
- Consistently argues with coworkers
- Belligerent toward customers/clients
- Consistently swears and curses at others
- Makes unwelcome sexual comments

Level 2

- Argues increasingly with customers, vendors, coworkers, and management
- Refuses to obey company policies and procedures
- Sabotages equipment and steals property for revenge
- Verbalizes wishes to hurt coworkers and/or management
- Sends sexual or violent notes to coworkers and/or management
- Sees self as victimized by management ("me" against "them" mentality)

Level 3

Frequent displays of intense anger resulting in:

- Recurrent suicidal threats
- Recurrent physical fights
- Destruction of property
- Use of weapons to harm others
- Commission of murder, rape, and/or arson

SOURCE: S. Baron (1993).

As can be seen from the progression of personal violence in this table, it is apparent that this person is a long-term employee. It takes some time for the employee to build up to the point where violent fatal behavior is manifested.

Victim Traits

The disgruntled employee does not kill for sexual reasons. He kills because the anticipated gain is psychological, and the reason or motivation is intrinsic to the personality of the killer—usually a perceived injustice. Unlike the lust serial killer, the disgruntled employee does not seek out an ideal victim type with certain physical traits, such as hair style or color, or body build. The physical characteristics of the victims are inconsequential. The victims are killed only because they happen to be around when the killer lets loose.

■   ■   ■   ■   ■   ■   ■   ■   ■   ■

Case Study: Joseph Wesbecker

On Thursday, September 14, 1989, at approximately 8:30 a.m., a disturbed and angry man went to his former place of employment. He had been placed on disability leave 7 months previously for severe psychiatric problems. He was armed with an AK-47, clips of ammunition, a SIG-Sauer 9mm semiautomatic assault pistol, two MAC-11 semiautomatic pistols, a bayonet, a .38-caliber Smith & Wesson revolver, and several hundred rounds of ammunition. The MAC-11s had been purchased only 4 days before. Joseph Wesbecker stepped onto the elevator of the Standard Gravure Printing Company, his former employer of more than 20 years. He walked from the elevator on the third floor. Sharon Needy, age 49, a receptionist, stood talking with another employee. She had gotten to work a little early that day to attend to some business, and she planned to take an extended lunch hour. She was the first one shot as Wesbecker opened fire. Her husband, George, said that he was told by the police that Wesbecker started shooting as soon as he stepped out of the elevator. Sharon happened to be at another workstation, and not her own (G. Needy, personal communication, May 10, 1998).

Lt. Jeff Moody, from the homicide unit of the Louisville, Kentucky Police Department, was one of the first police officers to respond to the scene. He remarked that when he and other officers entered the plant, they found blood and bodies scattered around the building. Moreover, they were not certain where Wesbecker was. After Wesbecker shot Needy, he shot another receptionist, Angela

Bowman, who survived. Walking through the hallways, Wesbecker fired randomly at anyone he saw. A few of the workers gathered together in one office and escaped detection. One worker, lying on the floor, heard some shots, and then there was silence. She dialed 911. The call went through the telephone system at 8:38 a.m. Within the next minute, more than a dozen calls went through the 911 system, calls asking for aid and protection from a crazed killer who was stalking the premises of the plant.

Murdered Victims of Joseph Wesbecker

Name	Age
Richard O. Bragger	54
William S. Gannet	46
James G. Husband	47
Paul S. Sale	60
Sharon L. Needy	49
James F. Wile, Sr.	56
Lloyd R. White	42

Wesbecker continued his killings. He encountered one fellow worker, a casual acquaintance, and told him to get away from him. Why Wesbecker did not shoot this man is unclear. By this time, word had circulated throughout the plant that Crazy Joe Wesbecker was shooting people (Holmes & Holmes, 1998). Many ran and escaped his uncontrolled rage.

Walking down the hallway into the bindery division, he shot and killed James Husband. He walked through a tunnel and down to the ground floor. He shot William Gannet, James Wile, and Lloyd White. In the basement, Wesbecker killed Richard Bragger and Paul Sale. He also shot 13 other workers, but fortunately, they survived. Finally, the last shot was fired. Wesbecker took his own life on the ground floor in the pressroom, only a short distance from Wile, one of his victims. He shot himself in the face with one of his pistols.

What kind of man would go into his place of employment of two decades and kill people who had no connection to his medical disability termination? There is no clear answer. But we do know that this was a carefully planned case of mass murder. Wesbecker started collecting his weapons about a year earlier. Did he start planning for his rampage a year before?

"Had this been a plotted, methodically planned situation that he finally brought to culmination, or did something happen to him to set him off? We haven't been able to find that," said Louisville homicide detective Sgt. Gene Waldridge, who interviewed Wesbecker's relatives and looked into his background. The police, who said Wesbecker suffered from manic depression, interviewed a psychiatrist he had been seeing, as well as at least 40 Standard Gravure workers, including Wesbecker's former bosses.

But Waldridge (1989) said, "The big question—Why?—more than likely will never, ever be answered. You can't talk to that person. You don't know what motivates them" (p. A1).

There were special stressors that compelled Wesbecker to shoot 20 people before finally ending his own life. He had been seeking psychiatric help for the past year, and he had been put on Prozac a month before his rampage. Years later, relatives of the victims sued the makers of Prozac, Eli Lilly, claiming that the drug caused Wesbecker to become a mass killer. The suit was judged in favor of Lilly.

Wesbecker, age 47, was apparently tormented by his leave from work. He thought that the company failed to compensate him for the time and the stress he had undergone on its behalf. He was angry at supervisors, and he told one fellow employee that if any supervisor came up to him, he would blow "out their brains" (Adams, Willis, & Scanlon, 1989). Wesbecker told other employees that he had thought about hiring someone to kill some of the people at the plant, and stated that he had plans to operate a remote-control model airplane with plastic explosives that he would guide through the plant to a determined destination. In addition, he told one fellow worker, "Me and old ack-ack will do a job that's been long overdue" (Adams et al., 1989, p. A16). Some workers acknowledged later that they should have taken his threats more seriously. He had a list of people whom he wanted dead. That list included both the executive vice president and the owner of the company. As one employee said, "You just figure he was mad at management. You figure it's just a way to get your frustration and your stress out. . . . You don't take it seriously" (Adams et al., 1989,

p. A16). Another fellow worker said that another employee told him about Wesbecker's explosives plan. He quickly dismissed Wesbecker as any danger, adding,

> I really didn't think he'd ever do anything. . . . I'm sure you've had people you work with talk about meeting a guy outside, punching him out or whatever. Well, maybe one out of every two or three hundred times it might happen. But most of the time a guy thinks about it five or 10 minutes and wonders why he ever made such a dumb remark. (Adams et al., 1989, p. A16)

Because Wesbecker's threats to his fellow workers were not taken seriously, they were never discussed with the supervisors at the plant. This made Wesbecker's eventual action more than a real possibility. Management could have gotten legal restraints barring Wesbecker from the premises, or other legal orders that possibly could have circumvented his actions.

Wesbecker is buried with his parents in a small Catholic cemetery in southern Indiana. St. Peter's Catholic Church held the mass of burial. The priest asked for forgiveness for the actions of this troubled man and a belief in the divine plan of God. But perhaps society needs a better plan of its own so that other innocent victims do not meet the same end. Early identification of troubled employees, psychological services given to needy employees, and other human services could become important interventions that may prevent the murder of innocent victims.

■   ■   ■   ■   ■   ■   ■   ■   ■   ■

CONCLUSION

There is no completely effective plan that will protect us from the acts of a disgruntled employee. This mass killer selects his victims randomly from among his fellow employees.

Among mass killers, the disgruntled employee is perhaps the most visible. The headlines are alive when such a case occurs. Our research for this book shows that family annihilators murder more victims, but most of the time, these murders are not reported on the front pages of the newspapers. Regardless, both types of mass killers will continue to commit senseless killings.

A possible proactive strategy is to develop a policy within the company or agency that a troubled employee would be encouraged to follow if the company suspects that he or she presents a danger to fellow workers. Employee education is an important part of any plan to prevent a mass murder of its most important asset, its employees.

REFERENCES

Abel, E. (1986). Childhood homicide in Erie County, New York. *Pediatrics, 77,* 709-713.

Adams, J., Willis, C., & Scanlon, L. (1989, September 16). Warnings of doom. *Courier Journal* (Louisville, KY), pp. A1, A16.

American Bar Association. (2000). *The American Bar Association's Commission on Domestic Violence Statistics and Prevalence Web Site* [On-line]. Available: www.abanet.org/domviol/stats.html

American Psychological Association. (1996). *Violence and the family: Report of the American Psychological Association Presidential Task Force on Violence and the Family.* Washington, DC: Author.

Barnard, G., Vera, H., Vera, M., & Newman, G. (1982). Till death do us part: A study of spouse murder. *Bulletin of the American Academy of Psychiatry and Law, 10,* 271-280.

Barnes, T. (1998, February). It's just a quarrel. *American Bar Association Journal,* p. 25.

Baron, L. (1993). Gender inequality and child homicide: A state level analysis. In A. Wilson (Ed.), *Homicide: The victim offender connection.* Cincinnati, OH: Anderson.

Baron, S. (1993). *Violence in the workplace: A prevention and management guide for business.* Ventura, CA: Pathfinder.

Bartholomew, A., Milte, K., & Galbally, F. (1978). Homosexual necrophilia. *Medicine, Science and the Law, 18,* 29-35.

Beirne, P., & Messerschmidt, J. (2000). *Criminology* (3rd ed.). Boulder, CO: Westview.

Bensimon, H. (1994). Violence in the workplace. *Training and Development,* pp. 27-32.

Bernick, B., & Spangler, J. (1985, September). Rovers kill up to 5,000 each year, experts say. *Desert News* (Las Vegas), p. A5.

Blackburn, D. (1990). *Human harvest: The Sacramento murder case.* New York: Knightsbridge.

Bourget, D., & Bradford, J. (1987). Fire, fetishism, diagnostic and clinical implications: A review of two cases. *Canadian Journal of Psychiatry, 32,* 459-462.

Boys accused in Columbine-like plot. (2000, April 15). *USA Today.* Available: www.usatoday.com/news/index/colo/colo161.htm.

Brill, A. (1941). Necrophilia. *Journal of Criminal Psychopathology, 2,* 51-73.

Bromberg, W. (1961). *The mold of murder: A psychiatric study of homicide.* Westport, CT: Greenwood.

Browne, A. (1986). Assault and homicide: When battered women kill. *Advances in Applied Psychology, 3,* 57-79.

Browne, A. (1987). *When battered women kill.* New York: Free Press.

Bugliosi, V. (1975). *Helter skelter: The true story of the Manson murders.* New York: Norton.

Bureau of Justice Statistics. (1989). *Report to the nation on crime and justice* (2nd ed.). Washington, DC: Government Printing Office.

Bureau of Justice Statistics. (1994a). *Bureau of Justice Statistics selected findings: Violence between intimates* (NCJ-149259). Washington, DC: U.S. Department of Justice, Office of Justice Programs.

Bureau of Justice Statistics. (1994b). *Special report: National Crime Victimization Survey, Violence Against Women* (NCJ-145325). Washington, DC: U.S. Department of Justice, Office of Justice Programs.

Bureau of Justice Statistics. (1995a). *National Crime Victimization Survey.* Washington, DC: U.S. Department of Justice, Office of Justice Programs.

Bureau of Justice Statistics. (1995b). *Special report: Violence against women: Estimates from the redesigned survey* (NCJ-154348). Washington, DC: U.S. Department of Justice, Office of Justice Programs.

Bureau of Justice Statistics. (1996). *Female victims of violent crime.* Washington, DC: U.S. Department of Justice, Office of Justice Programs.

Bureau of Justice Statistics. (1998). *Workplace violence 1992-1996* (Special Report 168634). Washington, DC: U.S. Department of Justice, Office of Justice Programs.

Bureau of Justice Statistics. (2000). *Homicide trends in the United States: Homicide victimization, 1950-1998* [On-line]. Available: www.ojp.usdoj.gov/bjs/homicide/totals.txt

Burg, B. (1992). The sick and the dead: The development of psychological theory on necrophilia from Kraft-Ebbing to the present. *Journal of History of the Behavioral Sciences, 218,* 242-254.

Busch, K., Zagar, R., Hughes, J., Arbit, J., & Bussell, R. (1990). Adolescents who kill. *Journal of Clinical Psychology, 46,* 472-485.

Buzawa, E., & Buzawa, C. (1990). *Domestic violence: The criminal justice response.* Newbury Park, CA: Sage.

Calef, V., & Weinshel, E. (1972). On certain equivalents of necrophilia. *International Journal of Psychoanalysis, 42,* 67-75.

Came, B., & Bergman, B. (1990). Victims in the home: Domestic violence in Quebec. *Canada,* p. 18.

Campion, J., Gravens, J., & Covan, F. (1988). A study of filicidal men. *American Journal of Psychiatry, 145,* 11-41.

Caputo, P. (1989, December). Death goes to school. *Esquire,* pp. 137-155.

Christoffel, K., Anzinger, N., & Amari, M. (1983). Homicide in childhood: Distinguishable patterns of risk related to developmental levels of victims. *American Journal of Forensic Medicine and Pathology, 4,* 129-137.

Christoffel, K., & Liu, K. (1983). Homicide death rates in childhood in 23 developed countries: U.S. rates atypically high. *Child Abuse & Neglect, 7,* 339-345.

Conklin, J. (1989). *Criminology* (3rd ed.). New York: Macmillan.

Conway, Z. (1989). Factors predicting verdicts in cases where battered women kill their husbands. *Law and Human Behavior, 13,* 253-269.

Copeland, A. (1985). Homicide in childhood: The Metro-Dade County experience from 1956-1982. *American Journal of Forensic Medicine and Pathology, 6,* 21-24.

Corder, B., Ball, B., & Hazlip, T. (1976). Adolescent patricide: A comparison with other adolescent murder. *American Journal of Psychiatry, 133,* 957-961.

Crazy Pat's revenge. (1986, September 1). *Time,* p. 19.

Crime: Murder by the numbers. (1985). *The Advocate, 697,* 31.

Cummings, S., & Monti, D. (1993). *Gangs.* Albany: State University of New York Press.

Dabbs, J., & Hargrove, M. (1997). Age, testosterone, and behavior among female inmates. *Psychomatic Medicine, 59,* 477-480.

Daly, M., & Wilson, M. (1988). *Homicide.* New York: Aldine de Gruyter.

Death on the playground. (1989, January 30). *Newsweek,* p. 35.

Dettlinger, C. (1983). *The list.* Atlanta, GA: Philmay.

Deykin, E., Levy, J., & Wells, V. (1987). Adolescent depression, alcohol and drug use. *American Journal of Public Health, 77,* 178-181.

Dietz, P. (1986). Mass, serial and sensational homicide. *Bulletin of the New York Academy of Medicine, 62,* 477-491.

D'Orban, P. (1990). Female homicide. *Irish Journal of Psychological Medicine, 7,* 64-70.

Duncan, J., & Duncan, G. (1971). Murder in the family: A study of some homicidal adolescents. *American Journal of Psychiatry, 127,* 1498-1502.

Eckert, A. (1985). *The scarlet mansion.* New York: Bantam.

Ellis, A. (1986). *The encyclopedia of sexual behavior.* New York: Hawthorne.

Ellis, H. (1946). *Psychology of sex.* New York: Jason Aronson.

Empey, L. (1978). *American delinquency.* Homewood, IL: Dempsey.

Ewing, C. (1997). *Fatal families.* Thousand Oaks, CA: Sage.

Faguet, R. (1980). Munchausen syndrome and necrophilia. *Suicide and Life Threatening Behavior, 10,* 214-218.

Farr, L. (1992). *The Sunset murders.* New York: Pocket.

Federal Bureau of Investigation. (1999). *FBI supplementary homicide report, 1976-1998.* Washington, DC: Government Printing Office. Available: www.ojp.usdoj.gov/bjs/homicide

Fishbain, D., Rao, V., & Aldrich, T. (1985). Female homicide-suicide perpetrators: A controlled study. *Journal of Forensic Science, 30,* 1148-1156.

Florida Governor's Task Force on Domestic and Sexual Violence. (1997). *Florida Mortality Review Project.* Tallahassee: Author.

Fox, J., & Zawitz, M. (1999). *Homicide trends in the United States.* Washington, DC: Government Printing Office.

Frankel, B. (1996, April 25). Safety and family clash in child welfare debate. *USA Today,* p. A1.

Freire, A. (1981). The necrophiliac character according to Erich Fromm: The case of Amanda. *Psiquis: Revista de Psiquiatria, Psicologia y Psicosomatica, 2,* 23-32.

Geberth, V. (1991). The lust murder: Psychodynamics of the killer and the psycho-social aspects of the crime. *Law and Order, 39*(6), 70-75.

Gelles, R. (1974). *The violent home: A study of physical aggression between husbands and wives.* Beverly Hills, CA: Sage.

Gelles, R., & Straus, M. (1985). Violence in the American family. In A. Lincoln & M. Straus (Eds.), *Crime in the family.* Springfield, IL: Charles C Thomas.

Gelles, R., & Straus, M. (1989). *Intimate violence: The causes and consequences of abuse in the American family.* New York: Simon & Schuster.

Goetting, A. (1987). Homicidal wives: A profile. *Journal of Family Issues, 8,* 332-341.

Goetting, A. (1989). Patterns of marital homicide: A comparison of husbands and wives. *Journal of Comparative Family Studies, 2,* 341-354.

Goetting, A. (1995). *Homicide in families and other special populations.* New York: Springer.

Gollmar, R. (1982). *Edward Gein: America's most bizarre murderer.* Delavan, WI: Charles Hallberg.

Greenfeld, L., & Snell, T. (1999). *Women offenders: Bureau of Justice Statistics special report* (Special Report 175688). Washington, DC: Bureau of Justice Statistics.

Hamm, M. (1993). *American skinheads: The criminology and control of hate crimes.* New York: Praeger.

Hansen, M., & Harway, M. (Eds.). (1993). *Battering and family therapy.* Newbury Park, CA: Sage.

Hawkins, D. (1986). *Homicide among Black Americans.* Lanham, MD: University Press of America.

Hazelwood, R., & Douglas, J. (1980). The lust murder. *FBI Law Enforcement Bulletin, 49,* 1-8.

Heide, K. (1998). *Young killers: The challenge of juvenile homicide.* Thousand Oaks, CA: Sage.

Heldman, K. (1999, June 28). *The Florida Hog Trail killings* [On-line]. Available: www.apbnews.com/crimesolvers/serialkiller/hogtrail/1999/06/28/hogtrail0628_01.html

Hickey, E. (1991). *Serial murderers and their victims.* Pacific Grove, CA: Brooks/Cole.

Hickey, E. (1997). *Serial murderers and their victims* (2nd ed.). Pacific Grove, CA: Brooks/Cole.

Hillbrand, M., Alexandre, J., & Young, J. (1997). Parricides: Characteristics of offender and victims, legal factors, and treatment issues. *Aggression and Violent Behavior, 4,* 179-190.

Holmes, R. (1983). *The sex offender and the criminal justice system.* Springfield, IL: Charles C Thomas.

Holmes, R. (1989). Inside the mind of the serial murderer. *American Journal of Criminal Justice, 13*(10), 2-18.

Holmes, R. (1990). Human hunters: A new type of serial killer. *Knightbeat, 9*(1), 43-47.

Holmes, R. (1991). *Sex crimes.* Newbury Park, CA: Sage.

Holmes, R., & DeBurger, J. (1985). Profiles in terror: The serial murderer. *Federal Probation, 53,* 53-59.

Holmes, R., & DeBurger, J. (1988). *Serial murder.* Newbury Park, CA: Sage.

Holmes, R., & Holmes, S. (1992). Understanding mass murder: A starting point. *Federal Probation, 56,* 53-61.

Holmes, R., & Holmes, S. (1999). School shootings: A country's concern. *Law and Order, 47*(6), 109-113.

Holmes, R. M., & Holmes, S. T. (1998). *Serial murder* (2nd ed.). Thousand Oaks, CA: Sage.

Holmes, S., Tewksbury, R., & Holmes, R. (1999). Fractured identity syndrome: A new theory of serial murder. *Journal of Contemporary Criminal Justice, 15,* 292-302.

Home Box Office. (1988). *Murder: No apparent motive.* HBO Special. Stanford, CT: Vestron Video.

Howard, M. (1986). Husband-wife homicide: An essay from a family law perspective. *Law and Contemporary Problems, 49,* 63-88.

Huff, R. (1996). *Gangs in America* (2nd ed.). Thousand Oaks, CA: Sage.

Humphrey, J., & Palmer, S. (1987). Stressful life events and criminal homicide. *Omega, 17,* 299-306.

Inciardi, J., Horowitz, R., & Pottieger, A. (1997). *Street kids, street drugs, street crime: An examination of drug use and serious delinquency in Miami.* Belmont, CA: Wadsworth.

Jenkins, P. (1988). Serial murder in England 1940-1985. *Journal of Criminal Justice, 16,* 1-15.

Katchadourian, H., & Lunde, D. (1975). *Fundamentals of human sexuality.* New York: Holt, Rinehart & Winston.

Kempe, C., Silverman, F., Steele, B., Droegemueller, W., & Silver, H. (1962). The battered child syndrome. *Journal of the American Medical Association, 181,* 17-24.

Kennedy, D., & Nolin, R. (1992). *On a killing day.* Chicago: Bonus Books.

Klein, M. (1995). The American street gang: Its nature, prevalence, and control. *Social Forces, 74,* 358-379.

Korbin, J. (1986). Childhood histories of women imprisoned for fatal child maltreatment. *Child Abuse & Neglect, 10,* 331-338.

Kratcoski, P. (1987). Families who kill. *Marriage and Family Review, 12,* 47-70.

Langlois, J. (1985). *Belle Gunness.* Bloomington: Indiana University Press.

Lester, D. (1987). Benefits of marriage for reducing the risk of violent death. *Psychological Reports, 61,* 198.

Lester, D. (1991). Murdering babies. *Social Psychiatry and Psychiatric Epidemiology, 26,* 83-85.

Levin, J., & Fox, J. (1985). *Mass murder.* New York: Plenum.

Lilly, J., Cullen, F., & Ball, R. (1989). *Criminological theory: Context and consequences.* Newbury Park, CA: Sage.

Lindedecker, C., & Burt, W. (1990). *Nurses who kill.* New York: Windsor.

Livesey, C. (1980). *The Manson women.* New York: Richard Marek.

Losey, J. (1994, February). Managing in an era of workplace violence. *Managing Office Technology,* pp. 27-28.

Lowenstein, L. (1989). Homicide: A review of recent research (1975-1985). *Criminologist, 13*(2), 74-89.

Lunde, D. (1977). *Murder and madness.* San Francisco: Jossey-Bass.

Maguire, K., & Pastore, A. L. (Eds.). (1999). *Sourcebook of criminal justice statistics.* Washington, DC: Government Printing Office.

Mann, C. (1984). *Female crime and delinquency.* Tuscaloosa: University of Alabama Press.

Mann, C. (1988). Getting even? Women who kill in domestic encounters. *Justice Quarterly, 5,* 33-51.

Mann, C. (1993). Maternal filicide of preschoolers. In A. Wilson (Ed.), *Homicide: The victim–offender connection.* Cincinnati, OH: Anderson.

Marzuk, P., Tradiff, K., & Hirsch, C. (1992). The epidemiology of murder-suicide. *Journal of the American Medical Association, 267*(23), 98-102.

Mashberg, T. (2000, April 16). Columbine multiplies public's fears—Schools deemed less safe. *The Boston Globe,* p. 4.

Masters, R., & Robertson, C. (1990). *Inside criminology.* Englewood Cliffs, NJ: Prentice Hall.

Mays, G. (1997). *Gangs and gang behavior.* Chicago: Nelson-Hall.

McGuire, C., & Norton, C. (1988). *Perfect victim.* New York: Dell.

McKnight, C., Mohr, J., & Quinsey, R. (1966). Mental illness and homicide. *Canadian Psychiatric Association Journal, 11,* 91-98.

The men who murdered. (1985). *FBI Law Enforcement Bulletin, 54*(8), 2-6.

Messner, S., & Tardiff, H. (1985). The social ecology of urban homicide: An application of the routine activities approach. *Criminology, 23,* 241-267.

Michaud, S., & Aynesworth, H. (1983). *The only living witness.* New York: Signet.

Mohr, J., Turner, R., & Jerry, M. (1964). *Pedophiles and exhibitionism.* Toronto: University of Toronto Press.

Money, J. (1984). Paraphilias: Phenomenology and classification. *American Journal of Psychotherapy, 38,* 164-179.

Moore, J. (1978). *Homeboys: Gangs, drugs, and prisons in the barrios of Los Angeles.* Philadelphia: Temple University Press.

Murphy, W. (1995). *Queer justice: Equal protection for victims of same-sex domestic violence.* 30 Val. U.L., Rev. 335.

Nash, J. (1980). *Murder, America: Homicide in the United States from the Revolution to the present.* New York: Evans.

Noguchi, T. (1985). *Coroner at large.* New York: Pocket.

Norris, J. (1988). *Serial killers: The growing menace.* New York: Kensington.

O'Boyle, T. (1992). Disgruntled workers intent on revenge increasingly harm colleagues and bosses. *Wall Street Journal,* pp. B1, B10.

O'Brien, R., Stockard, J., & Issacson, L. (1999). The enduring effects of cohort characteristics on age specific homicide rates, 1960-1995. *American Journal of Sociology, 104,* 1061-1095.

Pitt, S., & Bale, E. (1995). Neonaticide, infanticide and filicide: A review of the literature. *Bulletin of the American Academy of Psychiatry and Law, 23*(3), 379.

Podolsky, E. (1964). The chemistry of murder. *Pakistan Medical Journal, 15,* 9-14.

Police arrest students in school murder plots in Florida and California. (2000, April 15), *St. Louis–Post Dispatch,* p. 17. Associated Press.

Resnick, P. (1969). Child murder by parents. *American Journal of Psychiatry, 126,* 325-334.

Resnick, P. (1970). Murder of newborns. *American Journal of Psychiatry, 126,* 1414-1420.

Ressler, R., Burgess, A., & Douglas, J. (1988). *Sexual homicide: Patterns, motives and procedures for investigation.* New York: Free Press.

Revitch, E., & Weiss, R. (1962). The pedophilic offender. *Diseases of the Nervous System, 23,* 73-78.

Reynolds, B. (1990, August 30). This is the beginning of the end for murderer. *USA Today.*

Righton, P. (1981). The adult. In B. Taylor (Ed.), *Perspectives on pedophilia* (pp. 16-19). London: Batsford.

Rose, L. (1986). *Massacre of the innocents: Infanticide in Great Britain: 1800-1939.* London: Routledge & Kegan Paul.

Rosman, J., & Resnick, P. (1989). Sexual attraction to corpses: A psychiatric review of necrophilia. *Bulletin of the American Academy of Psychiatry and Law, 17,* 153-163.

Roth, J. (1994). *Understanding and preventing violence* (Research in Brief). Washington, DC: U.S. Department of Justice, National Institute of Justice.

Rule, A. (1983). *The stranger beside me.* New York: Signet.

Rule, A. (1988). *The I-5 killer.* New York: Signet.

Rush, G. (1991). *The dictionary of criminal justice* (3rd ed.). Guilford, CT: Dushkin.

Rush, G. (2000). *The dictionary of criminal justice* (5th ed.). New York: Dushkin/McGraw-Hill.

Rydelius, P. (1988). The development of antisocial behavior and sudden violent death. *Acta Psychiatrica Scandinavica, 77,* 398-403.

Scanlon, L., & Wolfson, A. (1989, September 15). Disturbed worker kills 7 and wounds 13 in rampage with AK-47 at Louisville plant. *Courier-Journal* (Louisville, KY).

Schechter, H. (1990). *Deranged.* New York: Pocket Books.

Schneider, M. (1998, December 1). Florida father charged in girl's death. *Chatta-nooga Free Press*, p. A6.

Schreiber, F. (1984). *The Shoemaker: The anatomy of a psychotic*. New York: Signet.

Seger, K. (1993). Violence in the workplace: An assessment of the problem based on responses from 32 large corporations. *Security Journal, 4*(3), 139-149.

Simpson, J. (1989, January 9). Beware of paper tigers. *Time*, pp. 104-105.

Slaughter in a school yard. (1989, January 30). *Time*, p. 29.

Smith, C., & Gullen, T. (1991). *The search for the Green River Killer*. New York: Penguin.

Smith, P. (1989). Perfect murders. *New Statesman and Society, 57*(2), 1-9.

Soler, E. (1987). Domestic violence is a crime: A case study of the San Francisco Family Violence Project. In D. Sonkin (Ed.), *Domestic violence on trial: Psychological and legal dimensions of family violence*. New York: Springer.

Spungen, D. (1998). *Homicide: The hidden victims*. Thousand Oaks, CA: Sage.

Stack, A. (1983). *The lust killer*. New York: Signet.

State v. Thornton, Tenn., 730 S.W.2d 309 (1987).

Stordeur, R., & Stille, R. (1989). *Ending men's violence against their partners: One road to peace*. Newbury Park, CA: Sage.

Swanson, C., Chamelin, N., & Terriro, L. (1996). *Criminal investigation* (6th ed.). New York: McGraw-Hill.

Sykes, G., & Matza, D. (1957). Techniques of neutralization: A theory of delinquency. *American Sociological Review, 22*.

10 minutes of madness. (1986, September 1). *Newsweek*, p. 18.

Topping, R. (1996, March 12). When "shaken baby" abuse is suspected. *Newsday*, p. A25.

U.S. Attorney General's Task Force on Family Violence. (1984, September). *Final report*. Washington, DC: Government Printing Office.

U.S. Commission on Civil Rights. (1982). *Under the rule of thumb: Battered women and the administration of justice*. Washington, DC: Government Printing Office.

Van Hoffman, E. (1990). *A venom in the blood*. New York: Donald I. Fine.

Virkunnen, L. (1981). The child as the participating victim. In M. Cook (Ed.), *Adult sexual interest in children*. London: Academic Press.

Waldridge, N. (1989, September 16). The big question—Why? *Courier Journal* (Louisville, KY), p. A1.

Walker, L. (1979). *The battered woman*. New York: Harper & Row.

Walker, L. (1983). The battered woman syndrome study. In D. Finkelhor, R. J. Gelles, G. Hotaling, & M. Straus (Eds.), *The dark side of families: Current family violence research*. Beverly Hills, CA: Sage.

Walker, L. (1984). *The battered woman syndrome*. New York: Springer.

Walker, L. (1989). *Terrifying love: Why battered women kill and how society responds*. New York: HarperCollins.

Walker, L. (1993). Legal self defense for battered women. In H. Hansen & M. Harway (Eds.), *Battering and family therapy: A feminist perspective*. Newbury Park, CA: Sage.

Weeks, J. (1986). *Sexuality*. New York: Ellis Horowitz.

Weiner, N., Zahn, M., & Sagi, R. (1990). *Violence: Patterns, causes and public policy*. New York: Harcourt Brace Jovanovich.

Whitehead, J., & Laub, S. (1989). *Juvenile justice: An introduction*. Cincinnati, OH: Anderson.

Whitmire, R. (1996, April 11). Child's death moves state closer to taking children from homes more quickly [On-line]. *Gannett News Service*. Available: web.lexus-nexus.com/universe

Wilbanks, W. (1983). The female offender in Dade County, Florida. *Criminal Justice Review, 8*(2).

Wilson, C., & Oden, R. (1987). *Jack the Ripper: Summing up and the verdict*. New York: Bantam.

Wolfgang, M., & Ferracuti, P. (1968). *The subculture of violence: Towards an integrative theory in criminology*. New York: Methuen.

Wolfgang, M., Thornberry, T., & Figlio, R. (Eds.). (1987). *From man to boy, from delinquency to crime*. Chicago: University of Chicago Press.

Wong, M., & Singer, K. (1973). Abnormal adolescents in Hong Kong. *Psychiatry, 123*, 295-298.

Wooden, W. (1995). *Renegade kids: Suburban outlaws*. Belmont, CA: Wadsworth.

Zorza, J. (1995). Mandatory arrest for domestic violence: Why it may prove the best first step in curbing repeat abuse. *Criminal Justice, 10*(33), 66-77.

INDEX

ABOUT THE AUTHORS

Ronald M. Holmes is Professor of Justice Administration at the University of Louisville. He is the author of several books, among them *Profiling Violent Crimes, Sex Crimes,* and *Serial Murder.* He is also the author of more than 50 articles appearing in scholarly publications. He is Vice President of the National Center for the Study of Unresolved Homicides and has completed more than 500 psychological profiles for police departments across the United States. He received his doctorate from Indiana University.

Stephen T. Holmes is Assistant Professor of Criminal Justice at the University of Central Florida. Prior to this position, he was a social science analyst for the National Institute of Justice in Washington, D.C. He has authored 6 books and more than 15 articles dealing with policing, drug testing, probation and parole issues, and violent crime. He received his doctorate from the University of Cincinnati.